Daisy Goodwin
Poems to Last a Lifetime

HarperCollins*Publishers*

Thank you

I have an embarrassing number of people to thank for helping me with this book: Ned Williams and Tabitha Potts for the poems and the strategic piles of paper; Versha Jones and Julian Humphries for the brilliant design; Caroline Michel for wanting to make it bigger and better; Michael Fishwick for his hard line on exclamation marks; Kate Hyde for her tact and patience and Alison Deboo for being on top of everything always.

HarperCollins*Publishers*
77–85 Fulham Palace Road
Hammersmith, London, W6 8JB
www.harpercollins.co.uk

Published by HarperCollinsPublishers 2004
9 8 7 6 5 4 3 2 1

Copyright © Daisy Goodwin 2004

The Author asserts the moral right to
be identified as the author of this work
Full permissions information may be found on pages 312–315

A catalogue record for this book
is available from the British Library

ISBN: 0-00-717707-0

Production Arjen Jansen
Designed by Versha Jones
Printed and bound in Singapore for Imago

contents

Foreword

Rummaging through a junk shop the other day I came across an album full of poems transcribed in meticulous italic handwriting. On the first page of the book was this dedication: 'For my darling daughter: words to sustain, support and console her when her mother cannot.' Judging from the poems, the album was put together sometime in the early 1900s – perhaps the daughter was getting married and moving away, perhaps the mother was ill and was compiling the book for her daughter as way of consoling her after her death. Whatever the motivation, the woman who compiled that album was the product of an age that took poetry seriously. She, like so many of her contemporaries, believed that poetry was an essential part of life: she was passing on her favourite poems much as a modern mother now might hand over her favourite recipes (in fact there was a recipe for plum jam in this collection tucked away between the Kipling and the Keats).

Finding that album made me consider the poems that I would put in a collection for my daughters – to comfort, encourage and console them – and so the notion for this book began to take shape. The poems in this book are arranged to follow the emotional road map of a human life; starting with childhood, moving on through the traumas of adolescence, to arrive at the serial destinations of love, marriage, parenthood, the loss of love, ageing, bereavement; with detours into work, dieting, infidelity and bad hair days. My intention while compiling this book has been to provide such a wide variety of poems that whatever life has to throw at you there will be words here to make sense of it. Because, as that long dead Victorian mother knew, great poetry has the power to transform our lives. As the great American poet and novelist John Updike puts it, 'poetry should be illuminating, precise and make us feel a little better about the world we live in.'

I hope you will use this book as a recipe book for the mind; turning to it when you need some advice on how to grow up, or maybe some tips on dealing with your children growing up, looking to it for consolation when the phone doesn't ring or for inspiration when you are trying to do the right thing, consulting it for words that set the mood for weddings and funerals, reaching for it for reassurance when you find a new wrinkle, an extra pound or even a suspicious lump; – or you might even take it to bed to read for sheer pleasure. I can think of no better fate for this book than for it to be used and abused: stained with wine, tears and marmite sandwiches like a really well-loved cookery book.

Some of the poems here may be familiar, some of them will be new; there are poems here from twelfth-century Japan and twenty-first-century Ohio – but the one thing all these poems have in common is that they shed light on the world we live in. These are the poems that a hundred years ago I would have written out for my daughters.
They are poems, I think, that will last a lifetime. I hope when you read them that you feel the same way.

Daisy Goodwin
www.daisygoodwin.co.uk

From **Ithaka**
C. P. Cavafy

As you set out for Ithaka
hope your road is a long one,
full of adventure, full of discovery . . .

Keep Ithaka always in your mind.
Arriving there is what you're destined for.
But don't hurry the journey at all.
Better if it lasts for years,
so you're old by the time you reach the island,
wealthy with all you've gained on the way,
not expecting Ithaka to make you rich.

Ithaka gave you the marvellous journey.
Without her you wouldn't have set out.
She has nothing left to give you now.

And if you find her poor, Ithaka won't have fooled you.
Wise as you will have become, so full of experience,
you'll have understood by then what these Ithakas mean.

The first time I heard this poem was at the memorial service for my favourite history teacher. It was a fitting tribute to a woman who enriched so many lives by teaching her pupils the pleasures of curiosity. Ithaka is the island that Odysseus took ten years to return to after the Trojan War. The story of his journey is the Odyssey. *Cavafy's message in the poem is that the point of life is not simply to reach a destination but to enjoy the journey.*

The Journey
Mary Oliver

One day you finally knew
what you had to do, and began,
though the voices around you
kept shouting
their bad advice –
though the whole house
began to tremble
and you felt the old tug
at your ankles.
'Mend my life!'
each voice cried.
But you didn't stop.
You knew what you had to do,
though the wind pried
with its stiff fingers
at the very foundations,
though their melancholy
was terrible.

It was already late
enough, and a wild night,
and the road full of fallen
branches and stones.
But little by little,
as you left their voices behind,
the stars began to burn
through the sheets of clouds,
and there was a new voice
which you slowly
recognized as your own,
that kept you company
as you strode deeper and deeper
into the world,
determined to do
the only thing you could do –
determined to save
the only life you could save.

The American poet Mary Oliver is one of my favourite modern poets. She is not afraid to tackle the big themes, but she does so in the most elegantly simple language. I always return to this poem when I feel pulled out of shape by the conflicting demands of family and work. It reminds me that the only thing I can really change is myself.

Child
Sylvia Plath

Your clear eye is the one absolutely beautiful thing.
I want to fill it with colour and ducks,
The zoo of the new

Whose names you meditate –
April snowdrop, Indian pipe,
Little

Stalk without wrinkle,
Pool in which images
Should be grand and classical

Not this troublous
Wringing of hands, this dark
Ceiling without a star.

Sylvia Plath wrote this poem in January 1963. Her marriage to Ted Hughes had fallen apart and she was living alone with her two small children. I think this poem poignantly captures every parent's desire to protect their children from the grim realities of life, what Plath calls the 'dark ceiling without a star'. Tragically, Plath was unable to insulate her children against the effects of her manic depression. She committed suicide shortly after writing this poem.

Infant Joy
William Blake

'I have no name:
I am but two days old.'

What shall I call thee?
'I happy am,
Joy is my name.'
Sweet joy befall thee!

Pretty Joy!
Sweet Joy, but two days old!
Sweet Joy I call thee,
Thou dost smile,
I sing the while,
Sweet joy befall thee!

This poem is taken from William Blake's Songs of Innocence. *Blake's own illustration shows a child cradled in its mother's arms inside a flower. It echoes the protective feelings we all have when cradling a new-born baby coupled with the wish to preserve that innocence for ever. Despite being happily married, Blake never had any children himself, which may be one of the reasons he writes about them with such wistful tenderness.*

Beatrix is Three
Adrian Mitchell

At the top of the stairs
I ask for her hand. O.k.
She gives it to me.
How her fist fits my palm,
A bunch of consolation.
We take our time
Down the steep carpetway
As I wish silently
That the stairs were endless.

When my eldest daughter was small and I was averaging maybe five hours' sleep a night, I remember seething with rage when well-meaning friends would say, 'Don't worry, it won't last for ever. They grow up so fast.' But now my daughter is thirteen, I am beginning to see what they meant. This poem by Adrian Mitchell captures every parent's regret that growing up must also mean growing away.

Child Development
Billy Collins

As sure as prehistoric fish grew legs
and sauntered off the beaches into forests
working up some irregular verbs for their
first conversation, so three-year-old children
enter the phase of name-calling.

Every day a new one arrives and is added
to the repertoire. You Dumb Goopyhead,
You Big Sewerface, You Poop-on-the-Floor
(a kind of Navaho ring to that one)
they yell from knee level, their little mugs
flushed with challenge.
Nothing Samuel Johnson would bother tossing out
in a pub, but then the toddlers are not trying
to devastate some fatuous Enlightenment hack.

They are just tormenting their fellow squirts
or going after the attention of the giants
way up there with their cocktails and bad breath
talking baritone nonsense to other giants,
waiting to call them names after thanking
them for the lovely party and hearing the door close.

The mature save their hothead invective
for things: an errant hammer, tire chains,
or receding trains missed by seconds,
though they know in their adult hearts,
even as they threaten to banish Timmy to bed
for his appalling behaviour,
that their bosses are Big Fatty Stupids,
their wives are Dopey Dopeheads
and that they themselves are Mr Sillypants.

*One of the most
disturbing things
about having
children is the
realisation that you
are the grown-up
now. I still haven't
really come to
terms with this,
especially when
my three-year-old's
tantrums seem
uncannily similar
to my own
behaviour. The
wonderful
American poet
Billy Collins clearly
has the same
problem.*

Timothy Winters
Charles Causley

Timothy Winters comes to school
With eyes as wide as a football pool,
Ears like bombs and teeth like splinters:
A blitz of a boy is Timothy Winters.

His belly is white, his neck is dark,
And his hair is an exclamation mark.
His clothes are enough to scare a crow
And through his britches the blue winds blow.

When teacher talks he won't hear a word
And he shoots down dead the arithmetic-bird,
He licks the patterns off his plate
And he's not even heard of the Welfare State.

Timothy Winters has bloody feet
And he lives in a house on Suez Street,
He sleeps in a sack on the kitchen floor
And they say there aren't boys like him any more.

Old Man Winters likes his beer
And his missus ran off with a bombardier,
Grandma sits in the grate with a gin
And Timothy's dosed with an aspirin.

The Welfare Worker lies awake
But the law's as tricky as a ten-foot snake,
So Timothy Winters drinks his cup
And slowly goes on growing up.

At Morning Prayers the Master helves
For children less fortunate than ourselves,
And the loudest response in the room is when
Timothy Winters roars 'Amen!'

So come one angel, come on ten:
Timothy Winters says 'Amen
Amen amen amen amen.'
Timothy Winters, Lord.
                    Amen.

The late, great Charles Causley is one of our most underrated poets. The emphatic rhyming scheme and the jolly, hym-like metre is an ironic counterpoint to the tragic fate of Timothy Winters.

The Lesson
Edward Lucie-Smith

'Your father's gone,' my bald headmaster said.
His shiny dome and brown tobacco jar
Splintered at once in tears. It wasn't grief.
I cried for knowledge which was bitterer
Than any grief. For there and then I knew
That grief has uses – that a father dead
Could bind the bully's fist a week or two;
And then I cried for shame, then for relief.

I was a month past ten when I learnt this:
I still remember how the noise was stilled
In school–assembly when my grief came in.
Some goldfish in a bowl quietly sculled
Around their shining prison on its shelf.
They were indifferent. All the other eyes
Were turned towards me. Somewhere in myself
Pride, like a goldfish, flashed a sudden fin.

Although this poem was written when the poet was an adult, it is a stunning evocation of the protective self-centredness of childhood. The boy in the poem pitilessly records the bewildering mixture of shame, relief and pride that overwhelms him on hearing of his father's death. It is a helpful reminder to over-anxious parents of just how unsentimental children can be.

Spring and Fall (to a young child)
Gerard Manley Hopkins

Márgarét, áre you gríeving
Over Goldengrove unleaving?
Leáves, líke the things of man, you
With your fresh thoughts care for, can you?
Áh! ás the heart grows older
It will come to such sights colder
By and by, nor spare a sigh
Though worlds of wanwood leafmeal lie:
And yet you *will* weep and know why.
    Now no matter, child, the name:
    Sórrow's spríngs áre the same.
    Nor mouth had, no nor mind, expressed
    What heart heard of, ghost guessed:
    It ís the blight man was born for.
    It is Margaret you mourn for.

In contrast to the last poem, here it is a child's hyper-sensitivity that is being recorded. Margaret is crying over the falling leaves. Hopkins makes the rather gloomy point that this is the first of many things she will cry for, that learning about mortality is an inevitable part of growing up. A poem to read when you are tempted to give your child a glib answer to the big questions of life.

A Wish for My Children
Evangeline Paterson

On this doorstep I stand
year after year
to watch you going

and think: May you not
skin your knees. May you
not catch your fingers
in car doors. May
your hearts not break.

May tide and weather
wait for your coming

and may you grow strong
to break
all webs of my weaving.

childhood

I wanted to have some poems in this book that were recipes for a happy life. Every parent wants passionately to protect their children from harm, but how many of us are capable of looking forward to the day when our children no longer need us?

Nine Mice
Jack Prelutsky

Nine mice on tiny tricycles
went riding on the ice,
they rode in spite of warning signs,
they rode despite advice.

The signs were right, the ice was thin,
in half a trice, the mice fell in,
and from their chins down to their toes,
those mice entirely froze.

Nine mindless mice, who paid the price,
are thawing slowly by the ice,
still sitting on their tricycles
. . . nine white and shiny *micicles*!

*The best way to encourage children to enjoy poetry is to read it aloud to them. This poem
makes my children laugh so much that they can barely get to the end without dissolving
into giggles.*

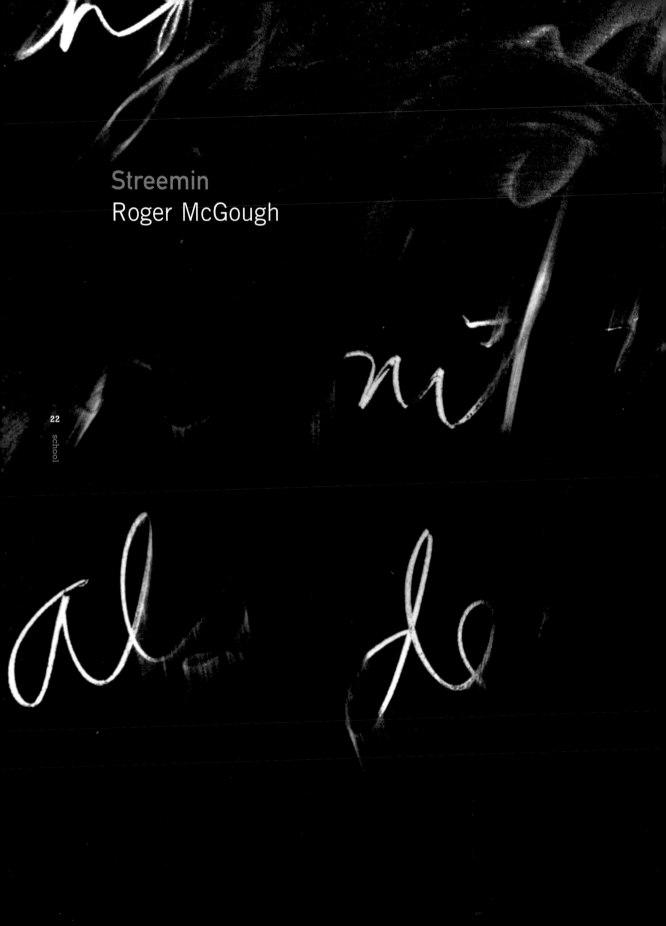

Streemin
Roger McGough

Im in the botom streme
which meens Im not brigth
Don't like reedin
Cant hardly ryt

but all these divishns
arnt reely fair
look at the cemtery
no streemin there

One of the few poets who writes as well for children as he does for adults, Roger McGough sums it all up here with 'Streemin'. Although 'Streemin' refers to the practice of putting children in different ability groups in a subject at school, the poem asks wider questions about the fairness of any system which divides human beings up and pretends that some are 'better' than others. Essential reading for parents and children around exam time.

The Road Not Taken
Robert Frost

Two roads diverged in a yellow wood,
And sorry I could not travel both
And be one traveller, long I stood
And looked down one as far as I could
To where it bent in the undergrowth;

Then took the other, as just as fair,
And having perhaps the better claim,
Because it was grassy and wanted wear;
Though as for that, the passing there
Had worn them really about the same,

And both that morning equally lay
In leaves no step had trodden black.
Oh, I kept the first for another day!
Yet knowing how way leads on to way,
I doubted if I should ever come back.

I shall be telling this with a sigh
Somewhere ages and ages hence:
Two roads diverged in a wood, and I —
I took the one less travelled by,
And that has made all the difference.

Frost wrote this famous poem after taking nature walks with his friend, the English poet Edward Thomas. Sometimes the two poets would plan a route but Thomas would later regret not taking a different path and sigh because he thought he had missed something wonderful. Frost found this amusing, not being the kind of man who believed in looking back. He wrote this poem shortly after returning to the USA and sent a copy to Thomas, thinking he would spot the reference to himself. Readers, however, assumed that the 'I' of the poem was Frost, and although he dropped clues in readings, Frost's audience tended not to see the poem's irony. Still, Frost always encouraged his readers to respect their personal responses to poems, so he had to accept that the poem has become many people's personal manifesto. It was recently voted America's favourite.

Leap Before You Look
W. H. Auden

The sense of danger must not disappear:
The way is certainly both short and steep,
However gradual it looks from here;
Look if you like, but you will have to leap.

Tough-minded men get mushy in their sleep
And break the by-laws any fool can keep;
It is not the convention but the fear
That has a tendency to disappear.

The worried efforts of the busy heap,
The dirt, the imprecision, and the beer
Produce a few smart wisecracks every year;
Laugh if you can, but you will have to leap.

The clothes that are considered right to wear
Will not be either sensible or cheap,
So long as we consent to live like sheep
And never mention those who disappear.

Auden was a poet, dramatist and librettist, one of the foremost intellectuals of the inter-war years. An undercurrent in many of his poems is his homosexuality, which obviously added to the risk of love during a less tolerant age. This may inform the poem, which is about the importance of embracing danger, otherwise we, as Auden puts it, 'consent to live like sheep'. This is the poem to read just before you tell your boss you need a six-month sabbatical.

Tiger

A. D. Hope

'At noon the paper tigers roar' Miroslav Holub

The paper tigers roar at noon;
The sun is hot, the sun is high.
They roar in chorus, not in tune,
Their plaintive, savage hunting cry.

O, when you hear them, stop your ears
And clench your lids and bite your tongue.
The harmless paper tiger bears
Strong fascination for the young.

His forest is the busy street;
His dens the forum and the mart;
He drinks no blood, he tastes no meat:
He riddles and corrupts the heart.

But when the dusk begins to creep
From tree to tree, from door to door,
The jungle tiger wakes from sleep
And utters his authentic roar.

It bursts the night and shakes the stars
Till one breaks blazing from the sky;
Then listen! If to meet it soars
Your heart's reverberating cry,

My child, then put aside your fear:
Unbar the door and walk outside!
The real tiger waits you there;
His golden eyes shall be your guide.

And, should he spare you in his wrath,
The world and all the worlds are yours;
And should he leap the jungle path
And clasp you with his bloody jaws,

Then say, as his divine embrace
Destroys the mortal parts of you:
I too am of that royal race
Who do what we are born to do.

Another poem about choice by the Australian poet Alec Hope. This poem is about the importance of finding your true passion in life and not being led astray by glamorous distractions. This poem should be on the National Curriculum.

Che Fece ... Il Gran Rifiuto

C. P. Cavafy

For some people the day comes
when they have to declare the great Yes
or the great No. It's clear at once who has the Yes
ready within him; and saying it,

he goes from honour to honour, strong in his conviction.
He who refuses does not repent. Asked again,

he'd still say no.
Yet that no – the right no –
drags him down all his life.

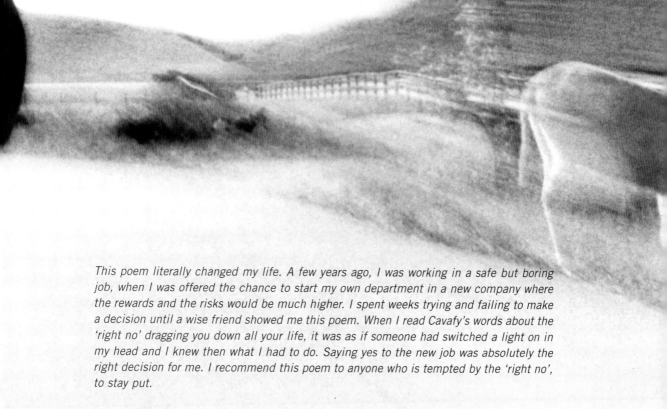

This poem literally changed my life. A few years ago, I was working in a safe but boring job, when I was offered the chance to start my own department in a new company where the rewards and the risks would be much higher. I spent weeks trying and failing to make a decision until a wise friend showed me this poem. When I read Cavafy's words about the 'right no' dragging you down all your life, it was as if someone had switched a light on in my head and I knew then what I had to do. Saying yes to the new job was absolutely the right decision for me. I recommend this poem to anyone who is tempted by the 'right no', to stay put.

First Love
John Clare

I ne'er was struck before that hour
With love so sudden and so sweet,
Her face it bloomed like a sweet flower
And stole my heart away complete.
My face turned pale a deadly pale,
My legs refused to walk away,
And when she looked, what could I ail?
My life and all seemed turned to clay.
And then my blood rushed to my face
And took my eyesight quite away,
The trees and bushes round the place
Seemed midnight at noonday.
I could not see a single thing,
Words from my eyes did start –
They spoke as chords do from the string,
And blood burnt round my heart.
Are flowers the winter's choice?
Is love's bed always snow?
She seemed to hear my silent voice,
Not love's appeal to know.
I never saw so sweet a face
As that I stood before.
My heart has left its dwelling-place
And can return no more.

Everyone remembers the first time they fell in love. This poem by the nineteenth-century poet John Clare perfectly sums up the heart-stopping, stomach-churning properties of young love. Most of us grow out of the intensity of those feelings, but not John Clare, who first caught sight of Mary Joyce when he was twelve and she was only eight; he wrote 'First Love' twenty-three years later! It might be worth adding that he was in an asylum at the time.

Casabianca

Love's the boy stood on the burning deck
trying to recite 'The boy stood on
the burning deck.' Love's the son
    stood stammering elocution
    while the poor ship in flames went down.

Love's the obstinate boy, the ship,
even the swimming sailors, who
would like a schoolroom platform, too,
    or an excuse to stay
    on deck. And love's the burning boy.

The American poet Elizabeth Bishop had a famously complicated romantic history
involving failed marriages and lovers of both sexes; but she put it all to good use. Poets
must belong to the only profession in the world that sees heartbreak as a career
opportunity. I particularly like this poem about the stubborn tenacity of true love.

She walks in beauty, like the night
Lord Byron

She walks in beauty, like the night
Of cloudless climes and starry skies,
And all that's best of dark and bright
Meets in her aspect and her eyes,
Thus mellow'd to that tender light
Which heaven to gaudy day denies.

One shade the more, one ray the less
Had half impair'd the nameless grace
Which waves in every raven tress
Or softly lightens o'er her face,
Where thoughts serenely sweet express
How pure, how dear their dwelling place.

And on that cheek and o'er that brow
So soft, so calm, yet eloquent,
The smiles that win, the tints that glow
But tell of days in goodness spent, –
A mind at peace with all below,
A heart whose love is innocent.

Byron dashed off this poem one morning, after catching a glimpse of his young cousin Anne Wilmot the night before. She was young and innocent, in direct contrast to the many women who were at that time plaguing him. It is one of his most beautiful lyrics; the kind of poem that made him the first poetic pin-up.

He Wishes for the Cloths of Heaven

W. B. Yeats

Had I the heavens' embroidered cloths,
Enwrought with golden and silver light,
The blue and the dim and the dark cloths
Of night and light and the half-light,
I would spread the cloths under your feet:
But I, being poor, have only my dreams;
I have spread my dreams under your feet;
Tread softly because you tread on my dreams.

When I first came across this poem at the age of fourteen, I fell in love with its luscious language and its mood of hopeless romantic masochism. Now I am older and wiser, I know better than to spread my dreams under anyone's feet. Yeats felt the same, commenting later that this poem was not the way to woo a woman. But every time I read this poem, I remember with pleasurable nostalgia the hopeless yearnings of my adolescence.

The Minute I Heard My First Love Story

Rumi (translated by Coleman Barks with John Moyne)

The minute I heard my first love story.
I started looking for you not knowing.
how blind that was.

Lovers don't finally meet somewhere.
They're in each other all along.

Rumi was born in 1207 in Balkh, Persia. Born into a wealthy family, his life changed when he became a Sufi mystic, a 'whirling dervish' as they were once known. Rumi's poems are immensely popular because of their simplicity and universality, despite the fact that his culture was so different from our own. A friend of mine read this poem to her husband on her wedding day; she said later that it perfectly expressed how she felt.

For Example
Erich Fried

Lots of things
can be laughable
such as
kissing my phone
when I have heard
your voice in it.

Not to kiss my phone
when I cannot kiss you
would be
still more laughable
and sadder.

Experience has taught me that falling in love and keeping one's dignity are mutually incompatible. Anyone who claims that they have never made a fool of themselves while in love is simply lying. Behaving foolishly goes with the territory, as this charming poem by the Austrian poet Erich Fried reminds us.

The Telephone
Maya Angelou

It comes in black
and blue, indecisive
beige. In red and chaperons my life.
Sitting like a strict
and spinstered Aunt spiked between my needs
and need.

It tats the day, crocheting
other people's lives
in neat arrangements
ignoring me
busy with the hemming
of strangers' overlong affairs or
the darning of my
neighbors' worn-out
dreams.

From Monday, the morning of the week,
through mid-times
noon and Sunday's dying
light. It sits silent.
Its needle sound
does not transfix my ear
or draw my longing to
a close.

Ring, Damn you!

missing you

Alexander Graham Bell's invention has been a boon for poets. This poem by Maya Angelou is about the frustration we all feel when waiting for the telephone to ring.

Warming Her Pearls
Carol Ann Duffy

Next to my own skin, her pearls. My mistress
bids me wear them, warm them, until evening
when I'll brush her hair. At six, I place them
round her cool, white throat. All day I think of her,

resting in the Yellow Room, contemplating silk
or taffeta, which gown tonight? She fans herself
whilst I work willingly, my slow heat entering
each pearl. Slack on my neck, her rope.

She's beautiful. I dream about her
in my attic bed; picture her dancing
with tall men, puzzled by my faint, persistent scent
beneath her French perfume, her milky stones.

I dust her shoulders with a rabbit's foot,
watch the soft blush seep through her skin
like an indolent sigh. In her looking-glass
my red lips part as though I want to speak.

Full moon. Her carriage brings her home. I see
her every movement in my head . . . Undressing,
taking off her jewels, her slim hand reaching
for the case, slipping naked into bed, the way

she always does . . . And I lie here awake,
knowing the pearls are cooling even now
in the room where my mistress sleeps. All night
I feel their absence and I burn.

Carol Ann Duffy was inspired to write this hummingly erotic poem by the way that ladies' maids used to increase the lustre of their mistresses' pearls by wearing them under their clothes, warming them against their skin. Duffy makes the pearls – scented, milky, warmed slowly with body heat – a symbol of the charged relationship between the two women and the focus of the maid's unfulfilled longing. The last words of the poem almost sizzle from the page.

Siren Song
Margaret Atwood

This is the one song
everyone would like
to learn: the song
that is irresistible:

In the Odyssey, the Sirens were bird-women who sang so beautifully that any man unfortunate enough to hear them could think of nothing else. Unfortunate, because setting foot on the Sirens' island meant certain death. Atwood's joke is that the secret of the irresistible siren song is really rather 'boring'. All the would-be siren has to do is to pose as a helpless maiden in need of rescue to get her man. Read this the next time you feel the urge to be irresistible, but remember to be careful what you wish for.

the song that forces men
to leap overboard in squadrons
even though they see the beached skulls
the song nobody knows
because anyone who has heard it
is dead, and the others can't remember
Shall I tell you the secret
and if I do, will you get me
out of this bird suit?
I don't enjoy it here
squatting on this island
looking picturesque and mythical
with these two feathery maniacs,
I don't enjoy singing
this trio, fatal and valuable.
I will tell the secret to you,
to you, only to you.
Come closer. This song
is a cry for help: Help me!
Only you, only you can,
you are unique

At last. Alas
it is a boring song
but it works every time.

Advice to Lovers
Frank O'Connor

The way to get on with a girl
Is to drift like a man in a mist,
Happy enough to be caught,
Happy to be dismissed.

Glad to be out of her way,
Glad to rejoin her in bed,
Equally grieved or gay
To learn that she's living or dead.

As in 'Siren Song', the actual advice given in this poem is to be treated with caution. But it is one of life's more irritating truths that men who are happy to drift in and out of a girl's life are always irresistible.

The Poetry of Dress
Robert Herrick

A sweet disorder in the dress
Kindles in clothes a wantonness: –
A lawn about the shoulders thrown
Into a fine distractión, –
An erring lace, which here and there
Enthrals the crimson stomacher, –
A cuff neglectful, and thereby
Ribands to flow confusedly, –
A winning wave, deserving note,
In the tempestuous petticoat, –
A careless shoe-string, in whose tie
I see a wild civility, –
Do more bewitch me, than when art
Is too precise in every part.

The seventeenth-century poet Robert Herrick's life was full of contradictions. Urbane and worldly, he nevertheless became a vicar in darkest Devon. He never married, but that did not stop him writing some of the most charming love poems in the English language. This is the poem to read if you are wondering what to wear on a date – think hippy chick, not Paris chic, and men will love you for it.

Meeting at Night
Robert Browning

The grey sea and the long black land;
And the yellow half-moon large and low;
And the startled little waves that leap
In fiery ringlets from their sleep.
As I gain the cove with pushing prow,
And quench its speed in the slushy sand.

In the early stages of a love affair, anticipation is all. I love this poem by the great Victorian poet Robert Browning about the heady moments leading up to the rapturous reunion between two lovers. Browning knew all about waiting. He courted Elizabeth Barrett, the woman who later became his wife, for two years as her father refused to allow her to marry. He wrote her poems on an almost daily basis, but this is one he did not send her. Perhaps he felt its sexual imagery (prow pushing into slushy sand!) might offend her delicate mid-Victorian sensibilities.

Then a mile of warm sea-scented beach;
Three fields to cross till a farm appears;
A tap at the pane, the quick sharp scratch
And blue spurt of a lighted match,
And a voice less loud, through its joys and fears,
Than the two hearts beating each to each!

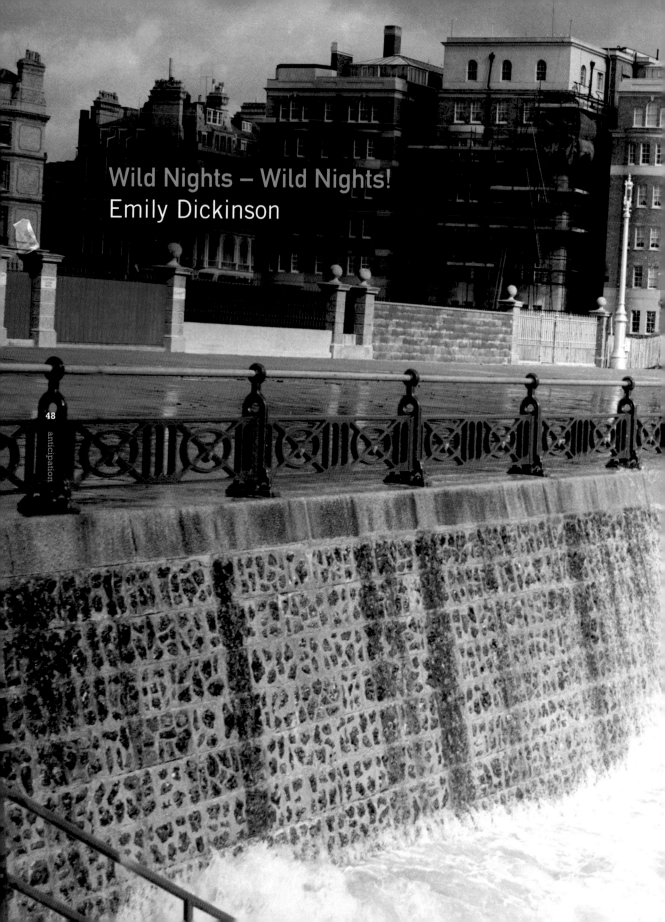

Wild Nights – Wild Nights!
Emily Dickinson

anticipation

Wild nights – wild nights!
Were I with thee,
Wild nights should be
Our luxury!

Futile the winds –
To a heart in port –
Done with the compass –
Done with the chart

Rowing in Eden!
Ah! the sea!
Might I but moor
Tonight In Thee!

This is the most astonishing poem – full of erotic yearning. What makes it even more remarkable is that the author, Emily Dickinson, was almost certainly a virgin and she had definitely never seen the sea.
When the 1891 edition of Dickinson's poems was being prepared, its editor wrote 'One poem I dread a little to print – that wonderful "Wild Nights" – lest the malignant read into it more than that virgin recluse ever dreamed of putting there.' But I find it unlikely that such a sexually charged poem was written by accident.

Love's Philosophy
Percy Bysshe Shelley

The fountains mingle with the river
And the rivers with the ocean,
The winds of heaven mix for ever
With a sweet emotion;
Nothing in the world is single,
All things by a law divine
In one another's being mingle –
Why not I with thine?

See the mountains kiss high heaven,
And the waves clasp one another;
No sister-flower would be forgiven
If it disdain'd its brother;
And the sunlight clasps the earth,
And the moonbeams kiss the sea –
What are all these kissings worth,
If thou kiss not me?

Poetry is full of persuasive arguments by eager young men intent on getting their beloveds into bed. I particularly like this playful poem by Shelley which tries to persuade his loved one that to resist his advances is to flout the laws of nature. Sadly for Shelley, the object of his poetic affections, Sophia Stacey, was very carefully chaperoned and all his flirting was in vain. A relief, perhaps, for Shelley's wife Mary.

The Sun Rising
John Donne

Busy old fool, unruly sun,
Why dost thou thus,
Through windows, and through curtains call on us?
Must to thy motions lovers' seasons run?
Saucy pedantic wretch, go chide
Late school-boys, and sour prentices,
Go tell court-huntsmen, that the King will ride,
Call country ants to harvest offices;
Love, all alike, no season knows, nor clime,
Nor hours, days, months, which are the rags of time.

Thy beams, so reverend and strong
Why shouldst thou think?
I could eclipse and cloud them with a wink,
But that I would not lose her sight so long:
If her eyes have not blinded thine,
Look, and tomorrow late, tell me,
Whether both th'Indias of spice and mine
Be where thou left'st them, or lie here with me.
Ask for those kings whom thou saw'st yesterday,
And thou shalt hear. All here in one bed lay.

She is all states, and all princes I,
Nothing else is.
Princes but play us; compared to this,
All honour's mimic; all wealth alchemy.
Thou sun art half as happy as we,
In that the world's contracted thus;
Thine age asks ease, and since thy duties be
To warm the world, that's done in warming us.
Shine here to us, and thou art everywhere,
This bed thy centre is, these walls, thy sphere.

I first read this poem at school and I remember being astonished, in my prudish sixteen-year old way, by its sexual candour. The poem follows a classical model, begging the sun to stay away and not wake the lovers after their night of bliss, but builds on it in characteristic style. You don't need to follow all the niceties of Donne's metaphysical conceit to appreciate this poem as a glorious celebration of sexual fulfilment. The last line, in particular, really brings home the way that passion creates its own little world.

Conviction

Stevie Smith

I like to get off with people,
I like to lie in their arms,
I like to be held and tightly kissed,
Safe from all alarms.

I like to laugh and be happy
With a beautiful beautiful kiss.
I tell you, in all the world
There is no bliss like this.

consummation

Stevie Smith's life was outwardly uneventful: she never married, and worked for thirty years as a secretary (her Novel On Yellow Paper *was given that title because she wrote it on yellow paper to distinguish it from her paid work) while living with her aunt in Palmer's Green. Her work, though, is always surprising and completely original, like this wonderful psalm for lovers.*

Contact lenses
Roger McGough

Somenights
she leaves them in
until after they have made love.
She likes to see clearly
the lines and curves of bodies.
To watch his eyes, his mouth.
Somenights she enjoys that.

Othernights
when taken by the mood
she takes them out before
and abandons herself
to her blurred stranger.
Other senses compete to compensate.
Without lenses, blindly accepts her fate.

consummation

Another poem about love fulfilled. 'Beer glasses' aren't just a myth (it's been scientifically proven that you can find someone more attractive after just one drink.) but the lady in this poem goes one better. In some moods she can surrender herself to an almost invisible lover and in others she can see clearly whatever is going on. What person with 20/20 vision can say the same?

Saturday Morning
Hugo Williams

Everyone who made love the night before
was walking around with flashing red lights
on top of their heads – a white-haired old gentleman,
a red-faced schoolboy, a pregnant woman
who smiled at me from across the street
and gave a little secret shrug,
as if the flashing red light on her head
was a small price to pay for what she knew.

Another post-coital poem, but this one is cheeky rather than languorous. Its author, Hugo Williams, is one of my favourite poets writing today. Read his limpid, personal poems if you want a completely unique take on life and love.

One Cigarette
Edwin Morgan

No smoke without you, my fire.
After you left,
your cigarette glowed on in my ashtray
and sent up a long thread of such quiet grey
I smiled to wonder who would believe its signal
of so much love. One cigarette
in the non-smoker's tray.
As the last spire
trembles up, a sudden draught
blows it winding into my face.
Is it smell, is it taste?
You are here again and I am drunk on your tobacco lips.
Out with the light.
Let the smoke lie back in the dark.
Till I hear the very ash
sigh down among the flowers of brass
I'll breathe, and long past midnight, your last kiss.

The Scottish Poet Laureate Edwin Morgan writes magnificent poems of requited love.
In this poem, the non-smoking narrator fondly contemplates the remains of his lover's
post-coital cigarette. The point he is making is that if you truly love someone, you love
everything about them – even their most annoying and unhealthy habits. Morgan
published this poem two years before 'coming out' at the age of seventy.

Sonnet 116
William Shakespeare

Let me not to the marriage of true minds
Admit impediments. Love is not love
Which alters when it alteration finds,
Or bends with the remover to remove:
O no! it is an ever-fixed mark
That looks on tempests and is never shaken;
It is the star to every wandering bark,
Whose worth's unknown, although his height be taken.
Love's not Time's fool, though rosy lips and cheeks
Within his bending sickle's compass come:
Love alters not with his brief hours and weeks,
But bears it out even to the edge of doom.
    If this be error and upon me proved,
    I never writ, nor no man ever loved.

This famous sonnet has been read at countless weddings, including mine, as a kind of manifesto for the resilience of true love. It is possible, though, to read the last two lines as an ironic counterpoint to the extravagant claims in the earlier part of the poem. How clever of Shakespeare to write a poem that works equally well for a wedding or a divorce.

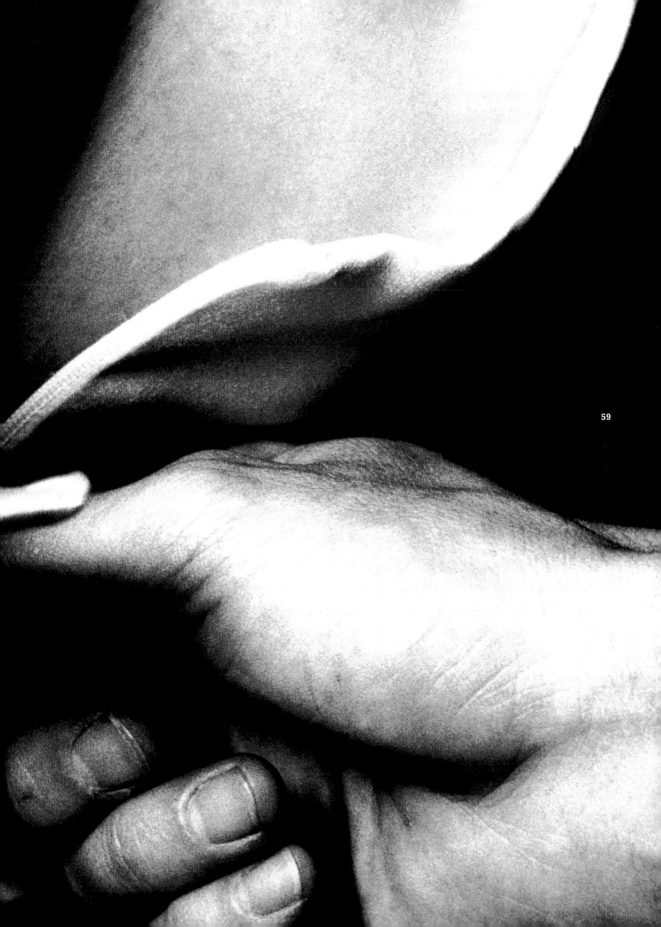

59

Love Poem
Vicki Feaver

Sharing one umbrella
We have to hold each other
Round the waist to keep together.
You ask me why I'm smiling –
It's because I'm thinking
I want it to rain forever.

This charming poem always reminds me of that blissful state at the beginning of a love affair when nothing, not even rain, can take the shine off the day.

from Sonnets from the Portuguese

Elizabeth Barrett Browning

How do I love thee? Let me count the ways.
I love thee to the depth and breadth and height
My soul can reach, when feeling out of sight
For the ends of Being and ideal Grace.
I love thee to the level of everyday's
Most quiet need; by sun and candle-light.
I love thee freely, as men strive for Right;
I love thee purely, as they turn from Praise.
I love thee with the passion put to use
In my old griefs, and with my childhood's faith
I love thee with a love I seemed to lose
With my lost saints, – I love thee with the breath,
Smiles, tears, of all my life! – and, if God choose,
I shall but love thee better after death

This touching sonnet was written by the Victorian poet Elizabeth Barrett Browning. She wrote it at the age of forty, shortly after meeting Robert Browning and falling in love with him. As a result, the poem is full of her astonishment and wonder about finding such a grand passion in adulthood. Robert Browning persuaded Elizabeth to publish this and the other Sonnets from the Portuguese *after their marriage. They became instantly and enduringly successful; this sonnet was recently voted the Nation's Favourite Love Poem.*

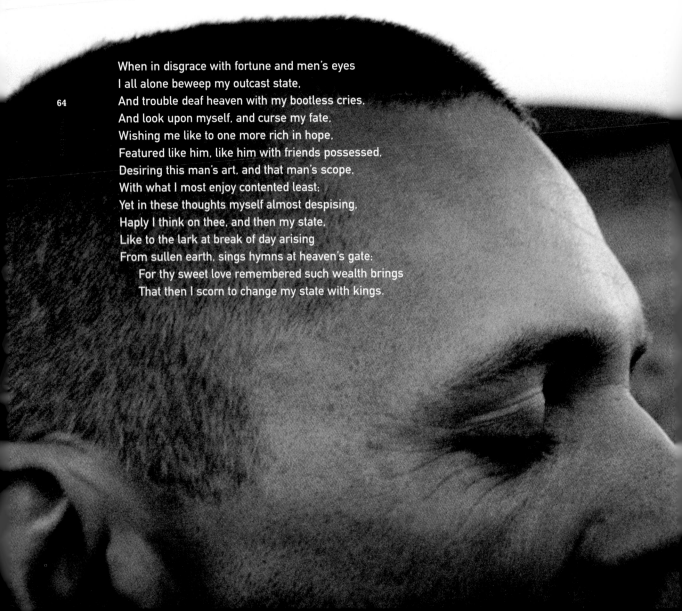

Sonnet 29
William Shakespeare

When in disgrace with fortune and men's eyes
I all alone beweep my outcast state,
And trouble deaf heaven with my bootless cries,
And look upon myself, and curse my fate,
Wishing me like to one more rich in hope,
Featured like him, like him with friends possessed,
Desiring this man's art, and that man's scope,
With what I most enjoy contented least;
Yet in these thoughts myself almost despising,
Haply I think on thee, and then my state,
Like to the lark at break of day arising
From sullen earth, sings hymns at heaven's gate;
    For thy sweet love remembered such wealth brings
    That then I scorn to change my state with kings.

There is nothing ambivalent about this sonnet. Any of us who are fortunate enough to love and be loved in return will appreciate Shakespeare when he says, 'For thy sweet love remembered such wealth brings/ That then I scorn to change my state with kings' – in other words, that no amount of worldly success or fame can be as valuable as your love is to me.

The Prophet

Kahlil Gibran

You were born together, and together you shall be forevermore.
You shall be together when the white wings of death scatter your days.
Ay, you shall be together even in the silent memory of God.
But let there be spaces in your togetherness.
And let the winds of the heavens dance between you.

Love one another, but make not a bond of love:
Let it rather be a moving sea between the shores of your souls.
Fill each other's cup but drink not from one cup.
Give one another of your bread but eat not from the same loaf.
Sing and dance together and be joyous, but let each one of you be alone.
Even as the strings of a lute are alone though
they quiver with the same music.

Give your hearts, but not into each other's keeping.
For only the hand of Life can contain your hearts.
And stand together yet not too near together:
For the pillars of the temple stand apart.
And the oak tree and the cypress grow not in each other's shadow.

Now You Will Feel No Rain
Apache song (translator unknown)

Now you will feel no rain,
for each of you will be a shelter to the other.

Now you will feel no cold,
for each of you will be warmth to the other.

Now there is no loneliness for you;
now there is no more loneliness.

Now you are two bodies,
but there is only one life before you.

Go now to your dwelling place,
to enter into your days together.

And may your days be good
and long on the earth.

true love

This is a traditional verse used by the Apache tribe at their wedding ceremonies. Simple but to the point. (Let's hope you can say the same for the best man's speech.)

As I Dig for Wild Orchids

Izumi Shikibu

(translated by Jane Hirshfield with Mariko Aratani)

As I dig for wild orchids
in the autumn fields,
it is the deeply-bedded root
that I desire,
not the flower.

I love the way that this poem from twelfth-century Japan compresses so much meaning into so few lines: real love is about finding what lies beneath the surface.

A Marriage

R. S. Thomas

We met
   under a shower
Of bird-notes.
      Fifty years passed,
Love's moment
         in a world in
Servitude to time.
            She was young;
I kissed with my eyes
            closed and opened
Them on her wrinkles.
            'Come', said death,
choosing her as his
            partner for
the last dance. And she,
      who in life
had done everything
      with a bird's grace,
opened her bill now
      for the shedding
of one sigh no
      heavier than a feather.

This poignant poem was written by the Welsh poet and clergyman R. S. Thomas after the death of his first wife. To call a fifty-year marriage 'love's moment' is a gauge of the merit of their relationship.

Only, from the long line of spray
Where the sea meets the moon-blanch'd land,
Listen! you hear the grating roar
Of pebbles which the waves draw back, and fling,
At their return, up the high strand,
Begin, and cease, and then again begin,
With tremulous cadence slow, and bring
The eternal note of sadness in.

Sophocles long ago
Heard it on the Aegean, and it brought
Into his mind the turbid ebb and flow
Of human misery; we
Find also in the sound a thought,
Hearing it by this distant northern sea.

The Sea of Faith
Was once, too, at the full, and round earth's shore
Lay like the folds of a bright girdle furl'd.
But now I only hear
Its melancholy, long, withdrawing roar,
Retreating, to the breath
Of the night-wind, down the vast edges drear
And naked shingles of the world.

Ah, love, let us be true
To one another! For the world, which seems
To lie before us like a land of dreams,
So various, so beautiful, so new,
Hath really neither joy, nor love, nor light,

Nor certitude, nor peace, nor help for pain;
And we are here as on a darkling plain
Swept with confused alarms of struggle and flight,
Where ignorant armies clash by night.

Love Poem
John Frederick Nims

My clumsiest dear, whose hands shipwreck vases,
At whose quick touch all glasses chip and ring,
Whose palms are bulls in china, burs in linen,
And have no cunning with any soft thing

Except all ill-at-ease fidgeting people:
The refugee uncertain at the door
You make at home; deftly you steady
The drunk clambering on his undulant floor.

Unpredictable dear, the taxi drivers' terror,
Shrinking from far headlights pale as a dime
Yet leaping before apoplectic streetcars –
Misfit in any space. And never on time.

*Having been teased from a tender age about my clumsiness (my nickname was Clumsina.)
I was delighted to discover this charming poem. I love the way that the poet contrasts his
wife's awkwardness of movement with the delicacy of her feelings for others.*

A wrench in clocks and the solar system. Only
With words and people and love you move at ease;
In traffic of wit expertly manœuvre
And keep us, all devotion, at your knees.

Forgetting your coffee spreading on our flannel,
Your lipstick grinning on our coat,
So gaily in love's unbreakable heaven
Our souls on glory of spilt bourbon float.

Be with me, darling, early and late. Smash glasses –
I will study wry music for your sake.
For should your hands drop white and empty
All the toys of the world would break.

Postscript for Gweno
Alun Lewis

If I should go away,
Beloved, do not say
'He has forgotten me.'
For you abide,
A singing rib within my dreaming side;
You always stay.

And in the mad tormented valley
Where blood and hunger rally
And Death the wild beast is uncaught, untamed,
Our soul withstands the terror
And has its quiet honour
Among the glittering stars your voices named.

Alun Lewis was a brilliant poet and short-story writer born in Wales. Gweno was his wife and great love. He wrote a poem for her the day he left to serve in World War II, called 'Goodbye': 'So we must say Goodbye, my darling, / And go, as lovers go, for ever'. He spent two years in active service, during which he wrote a great deal, but died in an accident in 1944. This is a wonderful and moving poem: what woman wouldn't want to be loved like this?

true love

The Skunk

Seamus Heaney

Up, black, striped and damasked like the chasuble
At a funeral mass, the skunk's tail
Paraded the skunk. Night after night
I expected her like a visitor.

The refrigerator whinnied into silence
My desk light softened beyond the veranda.
Small oranges loomed in the orange tree.
I began to be tense as a voyeur.

After eleven years I was composing
Love-letters again, broaching the word 'wife'
Like a stored cask, as if its slender vowel
Had mutated into the night earth and air

Of California. The beautiful, useless
Tang of eucalyptus spelt your absence.
The aftermath of a mouthful of wine
Was like inhaling you off a cold pillow.

And there she was, the intent and glamorous,
Ordinary, mysterious skunk,
Mythologized, demythologized,
Snuffing the boards five feet beyond me.

It all came back to me last night, stirred
By the sootfall of your things at bedtime.
Your head-down, tail-up hunt in a bottom drawer
For the black plunge-line nightdress.

This poem is about the skunk that used to visit Heaney some years ago when he was living in California. He is reminded of the animal when he sees his wife bent over the chest of drawers looking for her nightdress. Only a poet supremely sure of his craft, not to mention his marriage, would risk such a comparison. Heaney is clearly confident of both and the result is a richly comic love poem.

Eternity
William Blake

He who binds to himself a joy
Does the winged life destroy;
But he who kisses the joy as it flies
Lives in eternity's sun rise.

Blake was famously opposed to society's conventions. Although himself a devoted husband (he taught his wife to read and write) he disapproved of the way that society and the Church institutionalized human emotion. Today, I think this poem should be read as a warning against the dangers of possessiveness in a relationship.

Toads
Philip Larkin

Why should I let the toad work
Squat on my life?
Can't I use my wit as a pitchfork
And drive the brute off?

Six days of the week it soils
With its sickening poison –
Just for paying a few bills!
That's out of proportion.

Lots of folk live on their wits:
Lecturers, lispers,
Losers, loblolly-men, louts –
They don't end as paupers;

Lots of folk live up lanes
With fires in a bucket.
Eat windfalls and tinned sardines –
They seem to like it.

Their nippers have got bare feet,
Their unspeakable wives
Are skinny as whippets – and yet
No one actually starves.

Ah, were I courageous enough
To shout, Stuff your pension!
But I know, all too well, that's the stuff
That dreams are made on:

For something sufficiently toad-like
Squats in me, too;
Its hunkers are heavy as hard luck,
And cold as snow.

And will never allow me to blarney
My way of getting
The fame and the girl and the money
All at one sitting.

I don't say, one bodies the other
One's spiritual truth;
But I do say it's hard to lose either,
When you have both.

Despite achieving considerable success as a poet during his lifetime, Philip Larkin never gave up his day job as Chief Librarian of the Hull University Library. Clearly he needed both, and I think his poetry was the better for it. When Philip Larkin was asked 'How did you arrive upon the image of a toad for work or labour?' He replied, 'Sheer genius'.

The world is too much with us
William Wordsworth

The World is too much with us; late and soon,
   Getting and spending, we lay waste our powers:
   Little we see in Nature that is ours;
We have given our hearts away, a sordid boon!
This Sea that bares her bosom to the moon,
   The winds that will be howling at all hours
   And are up-gather'd now like sleeping flowers,
For this, for everything, we are out of tune;
It moves us not. – Great God! I'd rather be
   A pagan suckled in a creed outworn, –
So might I, standing on this pleasant lea,
   Have glimpses that would make me less forlorn;
Have sight of Proteus rising from the sea;
   Or hear old Triton blow his wreathèd horn.

It is hard to imagine Wordsworth, had he happened to live in the twenty-first century, settling down to a regular job in an office, although he might have found a berth at Greenpeace. I think this poem is a terrific antidote to the tsunamis of consumer frenzy that overwhelm us all at times.

Roman Wall Blues
W. H. Auden

Over the heather the wet wind blows,
I've lice in my tunic and a cold in my nose.

The rain comes pattering out of the sky,
I'm a Wall soldier, I don't know why.

The mist creeps over the hard grey stone,
My girl's in Tungria; I sleep alone.

Aulus goes hanging around her place,
I don't like his manners, I don't like his face.

Piso's a Christian, he worships a fish;
There'd be no kissing if he had his wish.

She gave me a ring but I diced it away;
I want my girl and I want my pay.

When I'm a veteran with only one eye
I shall do nothing but look at the sky.

It is easy to forget what a funny poet Auden could be when he chose. I have included this poem among others about work as a reminder that life could be a lot worse.

Managing the Common Herd:
two approaches for senior management
Julie O'Callaghan

THEORY X: People are naturally lazy.
They come late, leave early, feign illness.
When they sit at their desks
it's ten to one they're yakking to colleagues
on the subject of who qualifies as a gorgeous hunk.
They're coating their lips and nails with slop,
a magazine open to 'What your nails say about you'
Or 'Ten exercises to keep your bottom in top form'
under this year's annual report.
These people need punishment;
they require stern warnings
and threats — don't be a coward,
don't be intimidated by a batting eyelash.
Stand firm: a few tears, a Mars Bar,
several glasses of cider with her pals tonight
and you'll be just the same old
rat-bag, mealy-mouthed, small-minded tyrant
you were before you docked her
fifteen minutes' pay for insubordination.

Never let these con-artists get the better of you.

THEORY Z: Staff need encouragement.
Give them a little responsibility
and watch their eager faces lighting up.
Let them know their input is important.
Be democratic – allow all of them
their two cents' worth of gripes.
(Don't forget this is the Dr Spock generation.)
If eight out of twelve of them
prefer green garbage cans to black ones
under their desks, be generous –
the dividends in productivity
will be reaped with compound interest.
Offer incentives, show them
it's to their *own* advantage to meet targets.
Don't talk down to your employees.
Make staff believe that they
have valid and innovative ideas
and that not only are you interested,
but that you will act upon them.

Remember, they're human too.

You could spend two years of your life and a great deal of money going to business school,
or you could learn everything you need to know about managing people from this poem by
American-born Julie O'Callaghan.

Office Party
Alison Chisholm

I think I enjoyed the party.
I cannot remember it well.
My stomach is churning in circles
and my poor head is hurting like hell.

I think I enjoyed the buffet,
but the crab paste was long past its best.
The quiche was awash with heaven knows what
and the salad was limp and depressed.

The cheese cubes on sticks
were all crusted,
the vol-au-vents soggy and stale,
the trifle was dusted with fag ash
and smelt less of sherry than ale.

I think I enjoyed the fruit cup,
and a glass of the manager's wine.
The gin and the Scotch and the vodka
all left me feeling just fine.

The problems began with the brandy –
one sip of it went to my head.
I remember removing my stockings,
and then . . . oh, I wish I was dead.

I seem to remember the records,
they played all my favourite sounds.
I started the conga to 'Nights in White Satin'
and cha-cha'd to 'Send in the Clowns'.

Then somebody danced on the table
and sat on the manager's knee,
and did something crude with the manager's hat
and – oh glory, I think it was me.

My memory's starting to focus.
I remember the manager's face
when I told him I hated the work and the staff
and just what he could do with the place.

I think I enjoyed the party –
one over the eight is no crime,
but reviewing last night in the cold light of day,
I think I had better resign.

It is clearly not a good idea to get drunk at the office party, but an evening spent in the company of an orange juice and Reg from Accounts demonstrating his Mergers and Acquisitions is enough to make anyone reach for the Lambrusco.

I Meant to Do My Work Today
Richard LeGallienne

I meant to do my work today –
But a brown bird sang in the apple tree,
And a butterfly flitted across the field,
And all the leaves were calling me.

And the wind went sighing over the land
Tossing the grasses to and fro,
And a rainbow held out its shining hand –
So what could I do but laugh and go?

A contemporary of Oscar Wilde, LeGallienne was a remarkably prolific writer for someone whose famous poem was all about being distracted from the task in hand. Why not email this poem to your boss the next time the weather is beautiful and you don't fancy the office? Much more stylish than calling in sick.

Sea Fever
John Masefield

I must go down to the seas again, to the lonely sea and the sky,
And all I ask is a tall ship and a star to steer her by;
And the wheel's kick and the wind's song and the white sail's shaking,
And a grey mist on the sea's face, and a grey dawn breaking.

I must go down to the seas again, for the call of the running tide
Is a wild call and a clear call that may not be denied;
And all I ask is a windy day with the white clouds flying,
And the flung spray and the blown spume, and the sea-gulls crying.

I must go down to the seas again, to the vagrant gypsy life,
To the gull's way and the whale's way where the wind's like a whetted knife;
And all I ask is a merry yarn from a laughing fellow-rover,
And quiet sleep and a sweet dream when the long trick's over.

My grandmother used to read this poem to me when I was a child. It is one of those irresistible combinations of sound and meaning that makes any adventure seem possible.

Travel
Edna St. Vincent Millay

escape

A classic American poem, as America was at first a land of trains before it became a land of highways. Edna St Vincent Millay sums up the feeling of inexplicable restlessness that can overcome even the most settled person when they hear a train pass in the night. Of course, that's not a sound that many people hear nowadays, you are more likely to be woken up by it is more likely to be a Euro-juggernaut doing a three-point turn in your front garden.

The railroad track is miles away,
    And the day is loud with voices speaking,
Yet there isn't a train goes by all day
    But I hear its whistle shrieking.

All night there isn't a train goes by,
    Though the night is still for sleep and dreaming,
But I see its cinders red on the sky,
    And hear its engine steaming.

My heart is warm with the friends I make,
    And better friends I'll not be knowing;
Yet there isn't a train I wouldn't take,
    No matter where it's going.

Wild Geese
Mary Oliver

You do not have to be good.
You do not have to walk on your knees
for a hundred miles through the desert, repenting.
You only have to let the soft animal of your body
            love what it loves.
Tell me about despair, yours, and I will tell you mine.
Meanwhile the world goes on.
Meanwhile the sun and the clear pebbles of the rain
are moving across the landscapes,
over the prairies and the deep trees,
the mountains and the rivers.

Meanwhile the wild geese, high in the clean blue air,
are heading home again.
Whoever you are, no matter how lonely,
the world offers itself to your imagination,
calls to you like the wild geese, harsh and exciting –
over and over announcing your place
in the family of things.

You do not have to travel the world to get away from your troubles. This poem by Mary Oliver is a reminder that sometimes all you have to do is something really simple – like looking up at the sky – to find that crucial change of perspective.

On First Looking Into Chapman's Homer
John Keats

Much have I travell'd in the realms of gold.
　　And many goodly states and kingdoms seen;
　　Round many western islands have I been
Which bards in fealty to Apollo hold.
Oft of one wide expanse had I been told
　　That deep-brow'd Homer ruled as his demesne;
　　Yet did I never breathe its pure serene
Till I heard Chapman speak out loud and bold:
Then felt I like some watcher of the skies
　　When a new planet swims into his ken;
Or like stout Cortez when with eagle eyes
　　He star'd at the Pacific – and all his men
Look'd at each other with a wild surmise –
　　Silent. upon a peak in Darien.

Keats was not an aristocrat like Shelley or Byron, or middle-class like Coleridge or Wordsworth, but from a working-class background, something his critics at the time did not let him forget. His lack of learning in Greek was something that upset him and this is why his praise of Chapmans translation of Homer is so poignant. For someone like Keats, being given a good translation of the Odyssey *was literally a revelation, and this poem is a reminder of how much great literature can enrich one's life.*

Pied Beauty
Gerard Manley Hopkins

Glory be to God for dappled things –
    For skies of couple-colour as a brinded cow;
        For rose-moles all in stipple upon trout that swim;
Fresh-firecoal chestnut-falls; finches' wings;
    Landscape plotted and pieced – fold, fallow, and plough;
        And áll trádes, their gear and tackle and trim.

All things counter, original, spare, strange;
    Whatever is fickle, freckled (who knows how?)
    With swift, slow; sweet, sour; adazzle, dim;
He fathers-forth whose beauty is past change:

Praise him.

Gerard Manley Hopkins was a Jesuit priest whose innovation and brilliance as a poet were not greatly recognised during his lifetime. His poetry was deeply influenced by his studies in Anglo-Saxon: he limited his poetry to Anglo-Saxon rather than Roman or French derived English words and also tried to recapture the peculiar stresses and patterns ('sprung rhythm') of Anglo-Saxon verse in his own. The effect for anyone reading Hopkins now is how modern, lean and vivid his poetry feels. This poem is a glorious hymn to the Creation which can be appreciated by atheists, agnostics and believers alike.

From **The Garden**
Andrew Marvell

This is an extract describing the sensual pleasure of gardens: Marvell (the seventeenth-century Metaphysical poet best known for 'To His Coy Mistress') goes on to talk about the contemplative benefits of nature, how it can calm the mind, 'annihilating all that's made/ To a green thought in a green shade'. But what is most important here is the sense of renewal Marvell describes, something anyone with a patch of earth can understand. Marvell's metaphysical garden is full of exotic fruits, but the pleasure it affords will be familiar to the owner of the most humble allotment.

What wondrous life is this I lead!

Ripe apples drop about my head;
The luscious clusters of the vine
Upon my mouth do crush their wine;
The nectarine and curious peach
Into my hand themselves do reach;
Stumbling on melons, as I pass,
Insnared with flowers, I fall on grass.

From Glanmore Sonnets
Seamus Heaney

Dogger, Rockall, Malin, Irish Sea:
Green, swift upsurges, North Atlantic flux
Conjured by that strong gale-warning voice,
Collapse into a sibilant penumbra.
Midnight and closedown. Sirens of the tundra,
Of eel-road, seal-road, keel-road, whale-road, raise
Their wind-compounded keen behind the baize
And drive the trawlers to the lee of Wicklow.
L'Etoile, Le Guillemott, La Belle Hélène
Nursed their bright names this morning in the bay
That toiled like mortar. It was marvellous
And actual, I said out loud, 'A haven,'
The word deepening, clearing, like the sky
Elsewhere on Minches, Cromarty, The Faroes.

There is nothing more comforting on a night when sleep refuses to come than catching the soothing liturgy of the Shipping Forecast on the radio. Seamus Heaney pays tribute here to one of life's unexpected pleasures.

From *Endymion, Book 1*
John Keats

A thing of beauty is a joy for ever:
Its loveliness increases, it will never
Pass into nothingness; but still will keep
A bower quiet for us, and a sleep
Full of sweet dreams, and health, and quiet breathing.
Therefore, on every morrow, are we wreathing
A flowery band to bind us to the earth,
Spite of despondence, of the inhuman dearth
Of noble natures, of the gloomy days,
Of all the unhealthy and o'er-darkened ways
Made of our searching: yes, in spite of all,
Some shape of beauty moves away the pall
From our dark spirits.

simple pleasures

As Keats famously stated, 'Beauty is Truth, and Truth Beauty, that is all / Ye know on earth and all ye need to know'. Many critics have taken issue with this statement, but perhaps the fact that Keats's lines continue to be read and give pleasure to this day is enough to show that the poet understood the nature of immortality best.

Pippa's Song
Robert Browning

The year's at the spring,
And day's at the morn;
Morning's at seven;
The hill-side's dew-pearl'd;
The lark's on the wing;
The snail's on the thorn;
God's in His heaven –
All's right with the world!

This short poem is a lovely exercise in enjoying the moment. Browning is uniquely able to write in different voices: from the murderous but urbane husband in 'My Last Duchess' to the innocent Pippa in this poem. Although Browning may not have thought like Pippa himself, we can imagine from the happiness and sense of security implicit in the poem that he wished he did. If nothing else, this poem is a reason to get out of bed on a fine summer's morning.

The Lake Isle Of Innisfree
William Butler Yeats

I will arise and go now, and go to Innisfree,
And a small cabin build there, of clay and wattles made:
Nine bean-rows will I have there, a hive for the honey-bee,
And live alone in the bee-loud glade.

And I shall have some peace there, for peace comes dropping slow,
Dropping from the veils of the morning to where the cricket sings;
There midnight's all a-glimmer, and noon a purple glow,
And evening full of the linnet's wings.

I will arise and go now, for always night and day
I hear lake water lapping with low sounds by the shore;
While I stand on the roadway, or on the pavements grey,
I hear it in the deep heart's core.

*Yeats wrote this early poem during a period when he was interested in Thoreau's 'Walden',
published in 1854, the American writer's account of living alone in a hut in the woods in
Massachusetts for a year (although apparently his wife brought him lunch every day and
did his washing, something he omitted to mention).*
*The 'cabin' by the lake is described by a narrator who is far from Innisfree, where he spent
time in his youth, but plans to return. Yeats was in Fleet Street when the poem came to
him, and this poem will strike a chord with the millions of us who get through the miseries
of urban life sustained by an inner vision of escaping to the country one day.*

Leisure
W. H. Davies

What is this life if, full of care,
We have no time to stand and stare?

No time to stand beneath the boughs,
And stare as long as sheep and cows:

No time to see, when woods we pass,
Where squirrels hide their nuts in grass:

No time to see, in broad daylight,
Streams full of stars, like skies at night:

No time to turn at Beauty's glance,
And watch her feet, how they can dance:

No time to wait till her mouth can
Enrich that smile her eyes began?

A poor life this if, full of care,
We have no time to stand and stare.

W. H. Davies's autobiography was called the The Confessions of A Super Tramp *and, while he may not technically have been a vagrant, he certainly appeared to have spent a great deal of his time putting the philosophy of this poem into practice. What would he have thought of this poem being used on television to promote life insurance?*

Celia, Celia
Adrian Mitchell

When I am sad and weary
When I think all hope is gone
When I walk along High Holborn
I think of you with nothing on.

Adrian Mitchell wrote this poem about his wife Celia when he was working for the Evening Standard, *whose offices were then in Holborn. The poem became instantly popular and versions of it fill the Valentine's Day small ads of national newspapers. As Mitchell wrote, 'Readers began to take my poem and adjust the words to suit their own geography: When I am sad and weary/When I think all hope has gone/When I walk along Billericay High Street (or wherever) . . . Just like that, with no thought for the exacting prosodical demands entailed in the re-cutting of one of the crown jewels of twentieth-century English Literature, with no thought but for their steaming bestial desires!'*

'Hope' is the Thing with Feathers
Emily Dickinson

'Hope' is the thing with feathers –
That perches in the soul –
And sings the tune without the words –
And never stops – at all –

And sweetest – in the Gale – is heard –
And sore must be the storm –
That could abash the little Bird
That kept so many warm –

I've heard it in the chillest land –
And on the strangest Sea –
Yet, never, in Extremity ,
It asked a crumb – of Me.

Emily Dickinson wrote some nine hundred poems during her lifetime, but not one of them was published until 1890, years after her death. Not much is known about Dickinson's life; she lived quietly with her sister Lavinia in the house her grandfather Dickinson had built in Amherst, Massachussets until her death. But the poetry makes clear that this reclusive woman had known every degree of feeling (look back at 'Wild Nights' on page 48–9). This poem is about the irrepressible nature of hope – worth remembering the next time life seems unbearable.

I wandered lonely as a cloud
William Wordsworth

I wandered lonely as a cloud
That floats on high o'er vales and hills,
When all at once I saw a crowd,
A host, of golden daffodils;
Beside the lake, beneath the trees,
Fluttering and dancing in the breeze.

Continuous as the stars that shine
And twinkle on the milky way,
They stretched in never-ending line
Along the margin of a bay:
Ten thousand saw I at a glance,
Tossing their heads in sprightly dance.

The waves beside them danced; but they
Out-did the sparkling waves in glee:
A poet could not but be gay,
In such a jocund company:
I gazed – and gazed – but little thought
What wealth the show to me had brought:

For oft, when on my couch I lie
In vacant or in pensive mood,
They flash upon that inward eye
Which is the bliss of solitude;
And then my heart with pleasure fills
And dances with the daffodils.

simple pleasures

This is one of those poems that sums up something we have all felt far better than we will ever be able to do ourselves. Wordsworth's appreciation of nature had something of a spiritual awe in it, which comes through very strongly in his best poetry. Here, the sight of the daffodils becomes an inward vision that recurs to him again and again at other moments in his life, providing him with a constant source of delight. Wordsworth was famous for his long country rambles, a pleasure that busy urban people hardly know.

This is just to say
William Carlos Williams

I have eaten
the plums
that were in
the icebox

and which
you were probably
saving
for breakfast

Forgive me
they were delicious
so sweet
and so cold

This poem is so simple in its selfish hedonism and yet it suggests so much. It always reminds me of those notes that harassed couples leave each other on the kitchen table full of reminders about piano lessons and dry cleaning, but which are really all asking the same question, 'where are you when I need you?'

Against Dieting
Blake Morrison

Please, darling, no more diets.
I've heard the talk on why it's
good for one's esteem. I've watched you
jogging lanes and pounding treadmills.
I've even shed two kilos of my own.
But enough. What are love-handles
between friends? For half a stone
it isn't worth the sweat.
I've had it up to here with crispbread.
I doubt the premise too.
Try to see it from my point of view.
I want not less but more of you.

Some people put pictures of their pudgy selves in bathing suits on the fridge door as an incentive to lose weight. I think the long-suffering partners of irritable, halitosis-ridden low-carb dieters should retaliate with this poem.

The Health-Food Diner

Maya Angelou

No sprouted wheat and soya shoots
And Brussels in a cake,
Carrot straw and spinach raw,
(Today, I need a steak).

Not thick brown rice and rice pilau
Or mushrooms creamed on toast,
Turnips mashed and parsnips hashed,
(I'm dreaming of a roast).

Health-food folks around the world
Are thinned by anxious zeal,
They look for help in seafood kelp
(I count on breaded veal).

No Smoking signs, raw mustard greens,
Zucchini by the ton,
Uncooked kale and bodies frail
Are sure to make me run.

Loins of pork and chicken thighs
And standing rib, so prime,
Pork chops brown and fresh ground round
(I crave them all the time).

Irish stews and boiled corned beef
and hot dogs by the scores,
or any place that saves a space
For smoking carnivores.

The Skylight
Seamus Heaney

You were the one for skylights. I opposed
Cutting into the seasoned tongue-and-groove
Of pitch pine. I liked it low and closed,
Its claustrophobic, nest-up-in-the-roof
Effect. I liked the snuff-dry feeling,
The perfect, trunk-lid fit of the old ceiling.
Under there, it was all hutch and hatch.
The blue slates kept the heat like midnight thatch.

But when the slates came off, extravagant
Sky entered and held surprise wide open.
For days I felt like an inhabitant
Of that house where the man sick of the palsy
Was lowered through the roof, had his sins forgiven,
Was healed, took up his bed and walked away.

fresh starts

It is always easier to resist change, but even the 'right no' (compare the Cavafy poem on page 28–9) is an act of cowardice. Here, Seamus Heaney deftly compares a loft conversion with a New Testament miracle. The poet is saying that he didn't know what he was missing until this new perspective was opened up before him. (To sound a cautionary note: getting a radical new perspective on life is much easier and cheaper than a loft conversion and no planning permission is required.)

Wendy Cope

Yes, I agree. We'll pull ourselves together.
We eat too much. We're always getting pissed.
It's not a bad idea to find out whether
We like each other sober. Let's resist.
I've got the Perrier and the carrot-grater.
I'll look on a Scotch or a pudding as a crime.
We all have to be sensible sooner or later
But don't let's be sensible all the time.

No more thinking about a second bottle
And saying 'What the hell?' and giving in.
Tomorrow I'll be jogging at full throttle
To make myself successful, rich and thin.
A healthy life's a great rejuvenator
But, God, it's going to be an uphill climb.
We all have to be sensible sooner or later
But don't let's be sensible all the time.

The conversation won't be half as trivial –
You'll hold forth on the issues of the day –
And, when our evenings aren't quite so convivial,
You'll start remembering the things I say.
Oh, see if you can catch the eye of the waiter
And order me a double vodka and lime.
We all have to be sensible sooner or later
But I refuse to be sensible all the time.

There is beneficial change and then there is the kind of self-imposed torture that we all sporadically inflict upon ourselves. As someone who has detoxed and retoxed with embarrassing regularity, my new resolution is to read this poem whenever I feel the need to give things up.

This Be The Verse
Philip Larkin

They fuck you up, your mum and dad.
    They may not mean to, but they do.
They fill you with the faults they had
    And add some extra, just for you.

But they were fucked up in their turn
    By fools in old-style hats and coats
Who half the time were soppy-stern
    And half at one another's throats.

Man hands on misery to man.
    It deepens like a coastal shelf.
Get out as early as you can,
    And don't have any kids yourself.

Most people, when they have children, want to do a better job than their own parents. But parenting, as this famous poem by Larkin mordantly points out, is not a science where you can point proudly to progress. Larkin was quite consistent in his horror of family life

Pets and Death and Indoor Plants
Myron Lysenko

We're becoming old enough
to want to change our life-styles;
we're looking for substitutes
for sex & drugs and rock & roll.

But our dog . . . died
our cat . . . collapsed
budgies . . . wouldn't . . . budge.
Our roses . . . sank
our ferns . . . fizzled
cactus . . . carked it.

Yet, seated around roast dinners
our parents still talk about
the possibility of grandchildren.

Our minds . . . boggle
our bodies . . . fidget
our voices . . . falter

We're still immature
& we'd like to be
for a few years yet.

The world's not ready for our baby;
we're not ready for the world.
We're still trying to learn

how to make love properly;
still trying to come to terms
with pets & death & indoor plants.

commitment problems

There is apparently a new phenomenon: the quarter-century life crisis. So for anguished twenty-five-year-olds who don't know how to grow up, here is a themesong from Australian poet Myron Lysenko.

The Sorrow of Socks
Wendy Cope

Some socks are loners –
They can't live in pairs.
On washdays they've shown us
They want to be loners.
They puzzle their owners.
They hide in dark lairs.
Some socks are loners –
They won't live in pairs.

I believe a study recently found that some of those socks we lose in the wash really are disappearing into the innards of the washing machine . . . Whether this is the case, or whether they are just joining lost biros and house keys in some parallel dimension, who knows? Wendy Cope's poem applies equally well to socks and singletons, so I have put it here as an ode to the commitment phobic.

I'm Really Very Fond
Alice Walker

I'm really very
fond of you,
he said.

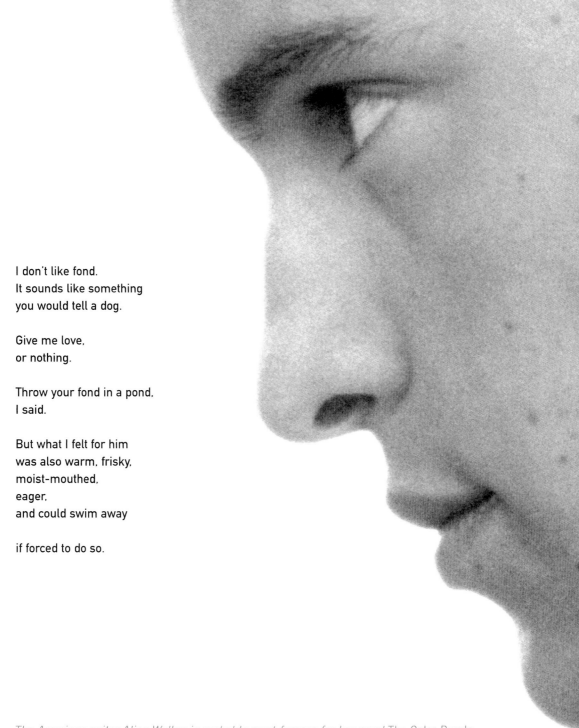

I don't like fond.
It sounds like something
you would tell a dog.

Give me love,
or nothing.

Throw your fond in a pond,
I said.

But what I felt for him
was also warm, frisky,
moist-mouthed,
eager,
and could swim away

if forced to do so.

The American writer Alice Walker is probably most famous for her novel The Color Purple *which became, as they say, a major motion picture. But she is also a very fine poet. I particularly like this poem about how easy it is to demand commitment from others when you don't really feel it yourself.*

Two Months Gone
Kate Clanchy

I suppose pregnancy is the closest we ever get to a state of enchantment. Kate Clanchy underlines the fairy-tale nature of early pregnancy, which as any parent knows is a long way from the squalling reality of birth.

It makes us want to shut all doors,
turn off the news, the phone, light
after light, pull the stairs, like a ladder,
up behind us, until, beneath the covers,
the darkness pressing around us,

we are the pair in the heart of the tale,
the woodsman who spared the unicorn,
the kitchen maid who hooked a witch
from the well and held her toe
through fourteen frightful incarnations,

and won, walked home with a wish
like a brimming glass of water, and when
the goblin with the question came,
sang out, to his single rhymed conundrum,
the answer: *all we ever wanted.*

In the black after the thunderclap, we wait
for the crooked town to wake, find
gilded roofs, loaves on each table,
for the crowds to come, half-dressed, incredulous,
for our fortune squalling in its cradle.

What I Learned From My Mother
Julia Kasdorf

I learned from my mother how to love
the living, to have plenty of vases on hand
in case you have to rush to the hospital
with peonies cut from the lawn, black ants
still stuck to the buds. I learned to save jars
large enough to hold fruit salad for a whole
grieving household, to cube home-canned pears
and peaches, to slice through maroon grape skins
and flick out the sexual seeds with a knife point.
I learned to attend viewings even if I didn't know
the deceased, to press the moist hands
of the living, to look in their eyes and offer
sympathy, as though I understood loss even then.
I learned that whatever we say means nothing,
what anyone will remember is that we came.
I learned to believe I had the power to ease
awful pains materially like an angel.
Like a doctor, I learned to create
from another's suffering my own usefulness, and once
you know how to do this, you can never refuse.
To every house you enter, you must offer
healing: a chocolate cake you baked yourself,
the blessing of your voice, your chaste touch.

parenthood

I recently came across this poem by a young American poet. I was particularly struck by the lines 'I learned that whatever we say means nothing / what anyone will remember is that we came'. This is a pretty good prescription for how to behave towards others at a time of crisis. The poet implies that this legacy from her mother can be an encumbrance, but I can think of no better inheritance.

Nettles

Vernon Scannell

My son aged three fell in the nettle bed.
'Bed' seemed a curious name for those green spears
That regiment of spite behind the shed:
It was no place for rest. With sobs and tears
The boy came seeking comfort and I saw
White blisters beaded on his tender skin.
We soothed him till his pain was not so raw.
At last he offered us a watery grin,
And then I took my hook and honed the blade
And went outside and slashed in fury with it
Till not a nettle in that fierce parade
Stood upright anymore. Next task: I lit
A funeral pyre to burn the fallen dead.
But in two weeks the busy sun and rain
Had called up tall recruits behind the shed:
My son would often feel sharp wounds again.

parenthood

Every parent will appreciate this poem about the poet's desire to take revenge on the
nettles that stung his son. Vernon Scannell had been, among many other things, a soldier
in World War II which may account for the military imagery that parades through this
poem. His real point, though, comes in the last line – we can wage war on nettles and put
safety locks on the windows, but we can never completely protect our children from harm.

Lullaby
Rosemary Norman

Go to sleep, Mum,
I won't stop breathing
suddenly in the night.

Got to sleep, I won't
climb out of my cot and
tumble downstairs.

Mum, I won't swallow
the pills that doctor gave you or
put hairpins in electric
sockets, just go to sleep.

I won't cry
when you take me to school and leave me
I'll be happy with other children
my own age.

Sleep, Mum, sleep.
I won't
fall in the pond, play with matches,
run under a lorry or even consider
sweets from strangers.

No, I won't
give you a lot of lip,
not like some.

parenthood

The ironic point of this poem is to suggest that the lullaby traditionally sung to children to help them get to sleep could sometimes be better directed towards the mother to help her cope with the stresses and strains of worrying about the safety and well being of her child.

I won't sniff glue,
fail my exams,
get myself/
my girlfriend pregnant.
I'll work hard and get a steady/
really worthwhile job.
I promise, I'll go to sleep.

I'll never forget
to drop in/phone/write
and if
I need any milk, I'll yell.

From **Alice in Wonderland**

Lewis Carroll

Speak roughly to your little boy,
And beat him when he sneezes:
He only does it to annoy
Because he knows it teases.

These lines are uttered by the Duchess in Lewis Carroll's Alice in Wonderland. *They are themselves a parody of a popular sentimental verse that starts, 'Speak gently to your little boy'. Carroll's poem encapsulates the feeling we sometimes get, as parents, that everything children do is with a view to winding us up, while at the same time showing how out of proportion to the offence our feelings of anger can be . . . Of course no one would take child-rearing tips from Carroll nowadays, but there is a certain wisdom in the cryptic utterances of his Wonderland characters.*

Carol Ann Duffy

I stood at the edge of my child's sleep
hearing her breathe;
although I could not enter there,
I could not leave.

Her sleep was a small wood,
perfumed with flowers;
dark, peaceful, sacred,
acred in hours.

And she was the spirit that lives
in the heart of such woods;
without time, without history,
wordlessly good.

I spoke her name, a pebble dropped
in the still night,
and saw her stir, both open palms
cupping their soft light;

then went to the window. The greater dark
outside the room
gazed back, maternal, wise,
with its face of moon.

Watching your children sleep is one of the rare (in my case, all too rare) privileges of parenthood, tenderly evoked here by one of our best living poets.

Walking Away
C. Day-Lewis

It is eighteen years ago, almost to the day –
A sunny day with the leaves just turning,
The touch-lines new-ruled – since I watched you play
Your first game of football, then, like a satellite
Wrenched from its orbit, go drifting away

Behind a scatter of boys. I can see
You walking away from me towards the school
With the pathos of a half-fledged thing set free
Into a wilderness, the gait of one
Who finds no path where the path should be.

That hesitant figure, eddying away
Like a winged seed loosened from its parent stem,
Has something I never quite grasp to convey
About nature's give-and-take – the small, the scorching
Ordeals which fire one's irresolute clay.

I have had worse partings, but none that so
Gnaws at my mind still. Perhaps it is roughly
Saying what God alone could perfectly show –
How selfhood begins with a walking away,
And love is proved in the letting go.

This poem should be read by every parent – it is about the realisation that one day your children will walk away from you and that your job is to let them go. C. Day-Lewis, who

At An Audition

Vicki Feaver

'Remember to smile darling,'

someone whispers, and there's a flurry
of hairbrushes – as if just one more polish
would make all the difference.
Then the children are gone:
scampering off white-socked like lambs.

It is the mothers who are nervous.
Left on their own they glance at magazines,
light cigarettes, or huddle together
against a wind that tells them
one day soon their darlings
will either disappoint or move beyond them.

129

Folding Sheets
Marge Piercy

They must be clean.
There ought to be two of you
to talk as you work, your
eyes and hands meeting.
They can be crisp, a little rough
and fragrant from the line;
or hot from the dryer
as from an oven. A silver
grey kitten with amber
eyes to dart among
the sheets and wrestle and leap out
helps. But mostly pleasure
lies in the clean linen
slapping into shape.
Whenever I fold a fitted sheet
making the moves that are like
closing doors, I feel my mother.
The smell of clean laundry is hers.

In this post-feminist age, housework remains a vexed issue, with some women happy to be domestic goddesses and others saying that all this talk of rediscovering housework is yet another way to make women feel guilty. But the American poet Marge Piercy talks about the pleasure of housework in the context of memory – how these tasks can link us to our mothers and their mothers.

On a Tired Housewife
Anon.

Here lies a poor woman who was always tired,
She lived in a house where help wasn't hired:
Her last words on earth were: 'Dear friends, I am going
To where there's no cooking, or washing, or sewing,
For everything there is exact to my wishes,
For where they don't eat there's no washing of dishes.
I'll be where loud anthems will always be ringing,
But having no voice I'll be quit of the singing.
Don't mourn for me now, don't mourn for me never,
I am going to do nothing for ever and ever.'

Sometimes Anon. says it all, and here she does. When you ask yourself 'How did women in my great-grandmother's time cope with raising six children, cooking, cleaning and managing the house without a dishwasher, washing machine or oven?' this poem gives the answer: with more than a little difficulty.

A Woman's Work
Dorothy Nimmo

Will you forgive me that I did not run
to welcome you as you came in the door?
Forgive I did not sew your buttons on
and left a mess strewn on the kitchen floor?
A woman's work is never done
and there is more.

The things I did I should have left undone
the things I lost that I could not restore;
Will you forgive I wasn't any fun?
Will you forgive I couldn't give you more?
A woman's work is never done
and there is more.

I never finished what I had begun,
I could not keep the promises I swore,
so we fought battles neither of us won
and I said 'Sorry!' and you banged the door.
A woman's work is never done
and there is more.

But in the empty space now you are gone
I find the time I didn't have before.
I lock the house and walk out to the sun
where the sea beats upon a wider shore
and woman's work is never done,
not any more.

*A woman I know recently left her husband after thirty years of unhappy marriage. I met
her six months later and she looked ten years younger. 'I have stopped blaming myself,'
she said. Here is a poem to give hope to anyone scared to be single.*

Farm Country
Mary Oliver

I have sharpened my knives, I have
Put on the heavy apron.

Maybe you think life is chicken soup, served
In blue willow-pattern bowls.

I have put on my boots and opened
The kitchen door and stepped out

Into the sunshine. I have crossed the lawn.
I have entered

The hen house.

A wickedly funny poem about the gap between urban fantasies of rural life and the visceral reality.

Atlas
U. A. Fanthorpe

There is a kind of love called maintenance,
Which stores the WD40 and knows when to use it;

Which checks the insurance, and doesn't forget
The milkman; which remembers to plant bulbs;

Which answers letters; which knows the way
The money goes; which deals with dentists

And Road Fund Tax and meeting trains,
And postcards to the lonely; which upholds

The permanently rickety elaborate
Structures of living; which is Atlas.

And maintenance is the sensible side of love,
Which knows what time and weather are doing
To my brickwork; insulates my faulty wiring;
Laughs at my dryrotten jokes; remembers
My need for gloss and grouting; which keeps
My suspect edifice upright in air;
As Atlas did the sky.

domestic bliss

There is an embarrassment of poems about marriages going wrong but strangely few about the mundane pleasures of long-term relationships. 'Atlas' by the splendid poet Ursula Fanthorpe is a much-needed hymn to the boring but crucial things that underpin lasting love.

Bloody Men
Wendy Cope

Bloody men are like bloody buses –
You wait for about a year
And as soon as one approaches your stop
Two or three others appear.

You look at them flashing their indicators,
Offering you a ride.
You're trying to read the destinations,
You haven't much time to decide.

If you make a mistake, there is no turning back.
Jump off, and you'll stand there and gaze
While the cars and the taxis and the lorries go by
And the minutes, the hours, the days.

The Perfect Match
Glyn Maxwell

There is nothing like the five minutes to go:
Your lads one up, your lads one down, or the whole
  Thing even. How you actually feel,
    What you truly know,
Is that your lads are going to do it. So,

However many times in the past the fact
Is that they didn't, however you screamed and strained,
  Pummelled the floor, looked up and groaned
    As the Seiko ticked
On, when the ultimate ball is nodded or kicked.

The man in the air is you. Your beautiful wife
May curl in the corner yawningly calm and true,
  But something's going on with you
    That lasts male life.
Love's one thing, but this is the Big Chief.

I include this poem for any football widow who has ever wondered whether she would win a match against the beautiful game for her man's affections. The answer, of course, is no.

Social Note
Dorothy Parker

Lady, lady should you meet
One whose ways are all discreet,
One who murmurs that his wife
Is the lodestar of his life,
One who keeps assuring you
That he never was untrue,
Never loved another one . . .
Lady, lady, better run!

Dorothy Parker was the blistering wit of the Algonquin literary circle and perhaps the quintessential New York poet in terms of sophistication and humour. Her romantic life, though, was a mess. As a result, her poems on the subject of love are unremittingly cynical. This poem is right on the money, as anyone who has been pounced on by Mr Happily Married will know.

Intimates
D. H. Lawrence

Don't you care for my love? she said bitterly.

I handed her the mirror, and said
Please address these questions to the proper person!
Please make all requests to head-quarters!
In all matters of emotional importance
please approach the supreme authority direct!
So I handed her the mirror.

And she would have broken it over my head,
but she caught sight of her own reflection
and that held her spellbound for two seconds
while I fled.

I am a great admirer of Lawrence's poetry. Not many English writers write with such honesty about sex and love. This savagely funny poem is typically candid about the narcissism that masquerades as love in so many relationships.

Man in Space
Billy Collins

All you have to do is listen to the way a man
sometimes talks to his wife at a table of people:
and notice how intent he is on making his point
even though her lower lip is beginning to quiver,

and you will know why the women in science
fiction movies who inhabit a planet of their own
are not pictured making a salad or reading a magazine
when the men from earth arrive in their rocket,

why they are always standing in a semicircle
with their arms folded, their bare legs set apart,
their breasts protected by hard metal disks.

The witty American poet laureate (2001–2) wrote this poem in a 'feminist moment', and it is certainly an interesting take on the battle of the sexes. Sometimes sci-fi tells us more about ourselves than we know, and here Collins refers back to all those old movies with women living on separate planets, which coincided with the birth of the feminist movement in the 1960s. However, it is the poem's beginning, where a man makes his wife cry over the dinner table, which is the most striking part of it for me.

A Story Wet as Tears
Marge Piercy

Remember the princess who kissed the frog
so he became a prince? At first they danced
all weekend, toasted each other in the morning
with coffee, with champagne at night
and always with kisses. Perhaps it was
in bed after the first year had ground
around she noticed he had become cold
with her. She had to sleep
with heating pad and down comforter.
His manner grew increasingly chilly
and damp when she entered a room.
He spent his time in water sports,
hydroponics, working on his insect
collection.
　　　　Then in the third year
when she said to him one day, my dearest,
are you taking your vitamins daily,
you look quite green, he leaped
away from her.
　　　　Finally on their
fifth anniversary she confronted him:
'My precious, don't you love me any
more?' He replied, 'Rivet, Rivet.'
Though courtship turns frogs into princes,
marriage turns them quietly back.

This poem is a sharp antidote to the soupy chick-lit dramas that always end with the girl discovering the true worth of her rough diamond. This is about what really happens next.

Flowers
Wendy Cope

Some men never think of it.
You did. You'd come along
And say you'd nearly brought me flowers
But something had gone wrong.

The shop was closed. Or you had doubts –
The sort that minds like ours
Dream up incessantly. You thought
I might not want your flowers.

It made me smile and hug you then.
Now I can only smile.
But look, the flowers you nearly brought
Have lasted all this while.

imperfect presents

Here Wendy Cope proclaims that the flowers her lover nearly bought, but rejected from a fear of cliché, are more precious and enduring than the real thing. But I have to say that I think Wendy may be alone in this. My advice to lovers who are worried about buying the wrong thing is to refer them to the words of Miss Lorelei Lee: 'square cut or pear shaped / these rocks don't lose their shape. Diamonds are a girl's best friend.' Or failing that, chocolate is always acceptable.

Monstrous Ingratitude
Boris Parkin

Gifts as gulfs . . .
Thoughts prompted by one
from ice ages ago:
a lime-green cardigan,
a garment I've never worn
and never will wear:
I hid it in a drawer
and mainly it stays there,
except when, as today,
on the trail of a lost sock,
I dig it up and feel once more
that sundering shock.

With kept creases
and buttons still done,
it invariably releases
the same terror as when
tearing the posh paper.
I saw at a glance
how little she understood me.
Well, I covered my inner silence
with mumbled thanks;
yet the rift persists
and even now
pride prevents me
from trying the thing on, somehow.

145

imperfect presents

It is a terrible admission, but getting the wrong present from someone who should know better is worse (almost) than getting nothing at all. This poem was written under a pseudonym by Christopher Reid, who clearly didn't want his wife to know how he really felt about that lime-green cardigan.

One Perfect Rose
Dorothy Parker

A single flow'r he sent me, since we met.
All tenderly his messenger he chose;
 Deep-hearted, pure, with scented dew still wet –
One perfect rose.

I knew the language of the floweret;
 'My fragile leaves,' it said, 'his heart enclose.'
Love long has taken for his amulet
 One perfect rose.

Why is it no one ever sent me yet
 One perfect limousine, do you suppose?
Ah no, it's always just my luck to get
 One perfect rose.

Dorothy Parker deconstructs the language of flowers and discovers that one perfect rose spells cheapskate. Which of us hasn't received a bouquet with the mental note 'Could do better', especially when the flowers that arrive are fresh from a garage forecourt, or a type we particularly hate? Of course, most of us wouldn't expect a 'perfect limousine', but perhaps a bunch of flowers is better than one – or none (see above).

Careless Talk
Mark Hollis

Bill
Was ill.

In his delirium
He talked about Miriam.

This was an error
As his wife was a terror

Known
As Joan.

As the famous World War II poster put it, 'Careless Talk costs lives'. Much better to go all theatrical and call everybody 'Darling!'.

Exposed on the cliffs of the heart
Rainer Maria Rilke

Exposed on the cliffs of the heart. Look, how tiny down there,
look: the last village of words and, higher,
(but how tiny) still one last
farmhouse of feeling. Can you see it?
Exposed on the cliffs of the heart. Stoneground
under your hands. Even here, though,
something can bloom; on a silent cliff-edge
an unknowing plant blooms, singing, into the air.
But the one who knows? Ah, he began to know
and is quiet now, exposed on the cliffs of the heart.
While, with their full awareness,
many sure-footed mountain animals pass
or linger. And the great sheltered bird flies, slowly
circling, around the peak's pure denial. – But
without a shelter, here on the cliffs of the heart . . .

A poem from the great German Romantic poet Rilke about the vertiginous nature of extreme emotion, where even words fail to give you a foothold.

Talking In Bed
Philip Larkin

Talking in bed ought to be easiest,

Lying together there goes back so far,
An emblem of two people being honest.

This is one of the most depressing poems in this book, but it is realistic in its bleakness. As so many of us have found out to our cost, it takes more than physical closeness to establish genuine intimacy. Larkin is writing here about his relationship with Monica Jones. They were lovers for most of their adult lives, but despite Monica's dogged devotion, Larkin could not bring himself to marry her and was serially unfaithful to her: unable, apparently, to be creative as a poet without the tensions of uncertain commitment and infidelity in his emotional life.

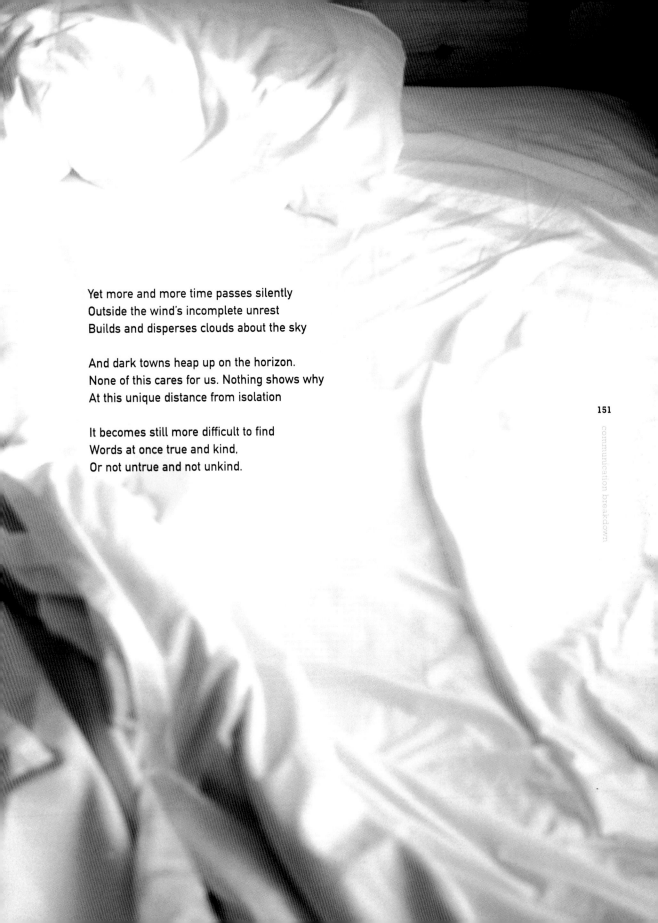

Yet more and more time passes silently
Outside the wind's incomplete unrest
Builds and disperses clouds about the sky

And dark towns heap up on the horizon.
None of this cares for us. Nothing shows why
At this unique distance from isolation

It becomes still more difficult to find
Words at once true and kind,
Or not untrue and not unkind.

Lullaby
W. H. Auden

Lay your sleeping head, my love,
Human on my faithless arm;
Time and fevers burn away
Individual beauty from
Thoughtful children, and the grave
Proves the child ephemeral:
But in my arms till break of day
Let the living creature lie,
Mortal, guilty, but to me
The entirely beautiful.

Soul and body have no bounds:
To lovers as they lie upon
Her tolerant enchanted slope
In their ordinary swoon,
Grave the vision Venus sends
Of supernatural sympathy,
Universal love and hope;
While an abstract insight wakes
Among the glaciers and the rocks
The hermit's carnal ecstasy.

Certainty, fidelity
On the stroke of midnight pass
Like vibrations of a bell,
And fashionable madmen raise
Their pedantic boring cry:
Every farthing of the cost,
All the dreaded cards foretell,
Shall be paid, but from this night
Not a whisper, not a thought,
Not a kiss nor look be lost.

Beauty, midnight, vision dies:
Let the winds of dawn that blow
Softly round your dreaming head
Such a day of welcome show
Eye and knocking heart may bless,
Find out mortal world enough;'
Noons of dryness find you fed
By the involuntary powers,
Nights of insult let you pass
Watched by every human love.

Another wonderful love poem from Auden, who writes so well about the fragility and paradoxical strength of love. He tells his lover to lay their head 'human on my faithless arm'. The assumption is that as we are all mortal, and weak, love may not last for ever but despite this his lover is 'to me, the entirely beautiful'.

Absence
William Shakespeare

Being your slave, what should I do but tend
Upon the hours and times of your desire?
I have no precious time at all to spend
Nor services to do, till you require:

Nor dare I chide the world-without-end hour
Whilst I, my sovereign, watch the clock for you,
Nor think the bitterness of absence sour
When you have bid your servant once adieu:

Nor dare I question with my jealous thought
Where you may be, or your affairs suppose,
But like a sad slave, stay and think of nought
Save, where you are, how happy you make those; –

So true a fool is love, that in your will
Though you do anything, he thinks no ill.

I love the languorous masochism of this poem, although I would shudder to find myself once more in that state of abject devotion it describes so accurately.

Non sum qualis eram bonae sub regno cynarae
Ernest Dowson

Last night, ah, yesternight, betwixt her lips and mine
There fell thy shadow, Cynara! thy breath was shed
Upon my soul between the kisses and the wine;
And I was desolate and sick of an old passion,
  Yea, I was desolate and bowed my head:
I have been faithful to thee, Cynara! in my fashion.

All night upon mine heart I felt her warm heart beat,
Night-long within mine arms in love and sleep she lay;
Surely the kisses of her bought red mouth were sweet;
But I was desolate and sick of an old passion,
  When I awoke and found the dawn was gray:
I have been faithful to thee, Cynara! in my fashion.

I have forgot much, Cynara! gone with the wind,
Flung roses, roses riotously with the throng,
Dancing, to put thy pale, lost lilies out of mind;
But I was desolate and sick of an old passion,
    Yea, all the time, because the dance was long:
I have been faithful to thee, Cynara! in my fashion.

I cried for madder music and for stronger wine,
But when the feast is finished and the lamps expire,
Then falls thy shadow, Cynara! the night is thine;
And I am desolate and sick of an old passion,
    Yea hungry for the lips of my desire:
I have been faithful to thee, Cynara! in my fashion.

Reading this poem is like walking in to a Victorian bordello, full of red plush, buxom girls and simmering guilt. The title is taken from a Latin poem and means 'I am not as I was under the rule of the good Cynara'. For me, it is richly evocative of the way people can let the memory of a past love undermine happiness in the present.

Story of a Hotel Room
Rosemary Tonks

BITTE NICHT
STÖREN
✳
PLEASE DO NOT
DISTURB
✳
PRIÈRE DE NE
PAS DÉRANGER

This poem should be read by anyone about to embark on an affair thinking that it's just a fling. It is much harder than you know to separate sex from love.

Thinking
we were safe
– insanity!

We went in to make love. All the same
Idiots to trust the little hotel bedroom.
Then in the gloom . . .
. . . And who does not know that pair of shutters
With the awkward hook on them
All screeching whispers? Very well then, in the gloom
We set about acquiring one another
Urgently! But on a temporary basis
Only as guests – just guests of one another's senses.

But idiots to feel so safe you hold back nothing
Because the bed of cold, electric linen
Happens to be illicit . . .
To make love as well as that is ruinous.
Londoner, Parisian, someone should have warned us
That without permanent intentions
You have absolutely no protection
– If the act is clean, authentic, sumptuous,
The concurring deep love of the heart
Follows the naked work, profoundly moved by it.

Mr and Mrs R and the Christmas Card List
Connie Bensley

Shall I cross them off?
It's twenty years since we last met.

of course Mr R and I once thought
we were made for each other –

Ah, that heart-stopping moment
by the kitchen sink, when he took off

his spectacles and fiercely kissed me.
But all that lasted less than a week

and what I recall more vividly
is Mrs R's good advice:

Always plunge your lemons in hot water
before you squeeze them.

One more year perhaps.

Infidelity seems so heart-stoppingly important at the time, but later, well, who knows . . .
Here is a rueful little poem about what is really important in life. As the saying goes,
'kissing don't last, cookery do'.

The Sick Rose
William Blake

O rose, thou art sick!
The invisible worm
That flies in the night,
In the howling storm,

Has found out thy bed
Of crimson joy,
And his dark secret love
Does thy life destroy.

One of Blake's most famous and enigmatic poems, whose apparent simplicity belies its layers of meaning. It is interesting to note that this poem from the Songs of Experience *is often thought, as a pair to one of the other Blake poems in this anthology 'Infant Joy' from the* Songs of Innocence. *I have placed it here among poems of adultery, as 'the bed of crimson joy' seems to me the most perfect description of those illicit pleasures.*

may i feel said he
E. E. Cummings

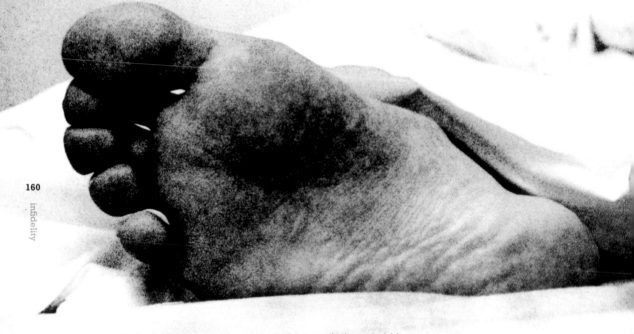

may i feel said he
(i'll squeal said she
just once said he)
it's fun said she

(may i touch said he
how much said she
a lot said he)
why not said she

(let's go said he
not too far said she
what's too far said he
where you are said she)

may i stay said he
(which way said she
like this said he
if you kiss said she

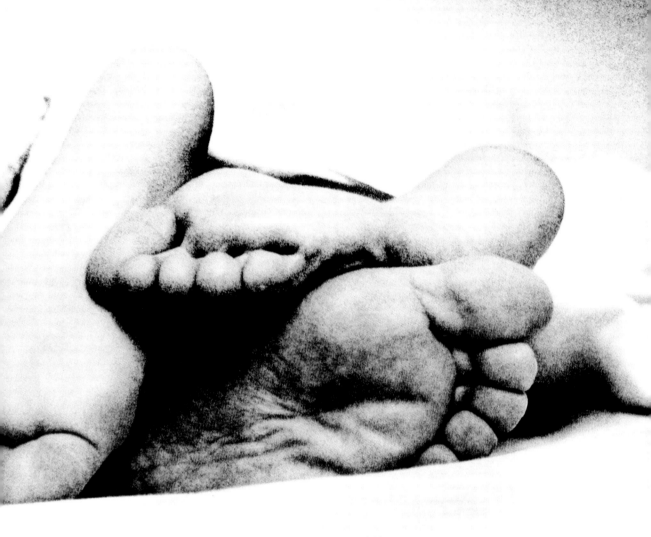

may i move said he
is it love said she)
if you're willing said he
(but you're killing said she

but it's life said he
but your wife said she
now said he)
ow said she

(tiptop said he
don't stop said she
oh no said he)
go slow said she

(cccome? said he
ummm said she)
you're divine! said he
(you are mine said she)

A witty, erotic poem about a breathless adulterous encounter. Brilliantly observed throughout, the last line should give pause to any man who thinks he can love 'em and leave 'em. Cummings had clearly read the Kipling poem where the 'female of the species is more deadly than the male'.

Taken in Adultery
Vernon Scannell

Shadowed by shades and spied upon by glass
Their search for privacy conducts them here,
With an irony that neither notices,
To a public house; the wrong time of year
For outdoor games; where, over a gin and tonic,
Best bitter and potato crisps, they talk
Without much zest, almost laconic,
Flipping an occasional remark.
Would you guess that they were lovers, this dull pair?
The answer, I suppose, is yes, you would.
Despite her spectacles and faded hair
And his worn look of being someone's Dad
You know that they are having an affair
And neither finds it doing them much good.
Presumably, in one another's eyes,
They must look different from what we see,
Desirable in some way, otherwise

Another cautionary tale about the dangers of adultery. Scannell wrote this poem in 1962
when he was living in Surrey. He later said it was not inspired by any one event – rather
it was the product of the wife-swapping commuter belt in which he lived. The biblical title
of the poem with its connotations of crime and punishment is in ironic contrast to the
banal liaisons of these suburban lovers.

They'd hardly choose to come here, furtively,
And mutter their bleak needs above the mess
Of fag-ends, crumpled cellophane and crumbs,
Their love feast's litter. Though they might profess
To find great joy together, all that comes
Across to us is tiredness, melancholy.
When they are silent each seems listening;
There must be many voices in the air:
Reproaches, accusations, suffering
That no amount of passion keeps elsewhere.
Imperatives that brought them to this room,
Stiff from the car's back seat, lose urgency;
They start to wonder who's betraying whom,
How it will end, and how did it begin –
The woman taken in adultery
And the man who feels he, too, was taken in.

Symptoms of Love
Robert Graves

Love is universal migraine,
A bright stain on the vision
Blotting out reason.

Symptoms of true love
Are leanness, jealousy,
Laggard dawns;

Are omens and nightmares –
Listening for a knock,
Waiting for a sign:

For a touch of her fingers
In a darkened room,
For a searching look.

Take courage, lover!
Could you endure such pain
At any hand but hers?

Scientists have recently classified love as a form of psychosis. Robert Graves knew all about this. The poet once threw himself out of a third-floor window after his mistress Laura Riding. Miraculously, they both survived.

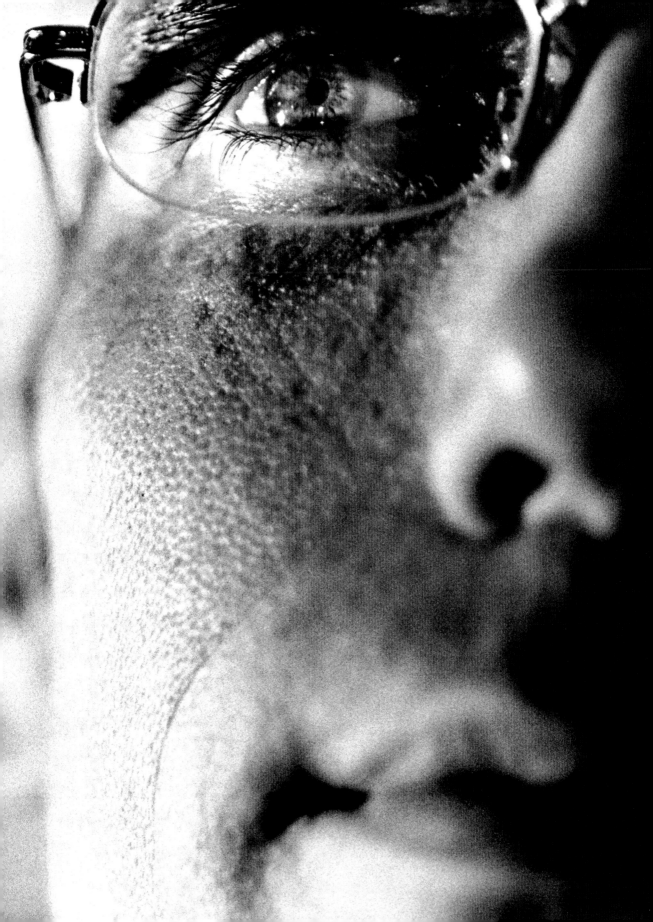

Defining the Problem
Wendy Cope

You could spend years in therapy trying to find out why it all went wrong. Or you could spend five minutes reading this poem. The choice is yours.

I can't forgive you. Even if I could
You wouldn't pardon me for seeing through you.
And yet I cannot cure myself of love
For what I thought you were before I knew you.

Will Not Come Back (After Becquer)
Robert Lowell

Dark swallows will doubtless come back killing
the injudicious nightflies with a clack of the beak;
but these that stopped full flight to see your beauty
and my good fortune . . . as if they knew our names –
they'll not come back. The thick lemony honeysuckle,
climbing from the earthroot to your window,
will open more beautiful blossoms to the evening;
but these . . . like dewdrops, trembling, shining, falling,
the tears of day – they'll not come back . . .
Some other love will sound his fireword for you
and wake your heart, perhaps, from its cool sleep;
but silent, absorbed, and on his knees,
as men adore God at the altar, as I love you –
don't blind yourself, you'll not be loved like that.

This free translation by Robert Lowell from a poem by a Sevillian poet is full of the menace that attends the extremes of desire. Potent, perfumed images are piled upon each other, but the real threat of the poem lies in the last two lines. Even at the height of his feelings, Lowell can see the end of the affair.

Jealousy
Rupert Brooke

When I see you, who were so wise and cool,
Gazing with silly sickness on that fool
You've given your love to, your adoring hands
Touch his so intimately that each understands,
I know, most hidden things; and when I know
Your holiest dreams yield to that stupid bow
Of his red lips, and that empty grace
Of those strong legs and arms, that rosy face,
Has beaten your heart to such a flame of love,
That you have given him every touch and move,
Wrinkle and secret of you, all your life,
— Oh! then I know I'm waiting, lover-wife,
For the great time when love is at a close,
And all its fruit's to watch the thickening nose
And sweaty neck and dulling face and eye,
That are yours, and you, most surely, till you die!
Day after day you'll sit with him and note
The greasier tie, the dingy wrinkling coat;
As prettiness turns to pomp, and strength to fat,
And love love, love to habit!

And after that,
When all that's fine in man is at an end,
And you, that loved young life and clean, must tend
A foul sick fumbling dribbling body and old,
When his rare lips hang flabby and can't hold
Slobber, and you're enduring that worst thing,
Senility's queasy furtive love-making,
And searching those dear eyes for human meaning,
Propping the bald and helpless head, and cleaning
A scrap that life's flung by, and love's forgotten, –
Then you'll be tired; and passion dead and rotten;
And he'll be dirty, dirty!

O lithe and free
And lightfoot, that the poor heart cries to see,
That's how I'll see your man and you! –

But you
– Oh, when that time comes, you'll be dirty too!

This poem about the corrosive nature of jealousy is by Rupert Brooke, a poet who is far better known for his patriotic lyrics like 'The Soldier'. The sulphurous tone of this work shows that he might have developed into a really great poet had he not died of fever while on active service in 1915.

Marriage a-la-mode
John Dryden

Why should a foolish marriage vow,
Which long ago was made,
Oblige us to each other now
When passion is decay'd?
We lov'd, and we lov'd, as long as we could,
Till our love was lov'd out in us both:
But our marriage is dead, when the pleasure is fled:
'Twas pleasure first made it an oath.

If I have pleasures for a friend,
And farther love in store,
What wrong has he whose joys did end,
And who could give no more?
'Tis a madness that he should be jealous of me,
Or that I should bar him of another:
For all we can gain is to give our selves pain,
When neither can hinder the other

after love

The most surprising thing about this postscript to a failed marriage is that it was written in the second half of the seventeenth century.

Past One O'Clock
Vladimir Mayakovsky

Past one o'clock. You must have gone to bed.

The Milky Way streams silver through the night.
I'm in no hurry; with lightning telegrams
I have no cause to wake or trouble you.
And, as they say, the incident is closed.
Love's boat has smashed against the daily grind.
Now you and I are quits. Why bother then
To balance mutual sorrows, pains and hurts.
Behold what quiet settles on the world.
Night wraps the sky in tribute from the stars.
In hours like these, one rises to address
The ages, history, and all creation.

The Russian poet Vladimir Mayakovsky started writing in prison, where he was serving time for political activity against the Tsarist regime. After the Revolution he drifted away from politics and devoted himself to poetry. These lines, about looking for serenity at the end of a love affair, were found on his body when he committed suicide in 1930. I find this poem almost unbearably beautiful.

For My Lover, Returning to his Wife
Anne Sexton

She has always been there, my darling.
She is, in fact, exquisite.
Fireworks in the dull middle of February
and as real as a cast-iron pot.

Let's face it, I have been momentary.
A luxury. A bright red sloop in the harbor.
My hair rising like smoke from the car window.
Littleneck clams out of season.

She is more than that. She is your have to have,
has grown you your practical, your tropical growth.
This is not an experiment. She is all harmony.
She sees to oars and oarlocks for the dinghy.

I give you back your heart.
I give you permission –

She is so naked and singular.
She is the sum of yourself and your dream.
Climb her like a monument, step after step.
She is solid.

As for me, I am a watercolor.
I wash off.

An extraordinary poem acknowledging the strange, intense, unspoken relationship between a mistress and her lover's wife. The last two lines are heartbreaking in their acknowledgement of the ephemeral nature of desire. Sexton, a contemporary of Sylvia Plath and a pupil of Robert Lowell, wrote searingly confessional poetry. Like Plath, she took her own life.

Voice
Ann Sansom

Call, by all means, but just once
don't use the *broken heart again* voice;
the *I'm sick to death of life and women
and romance* voice *but with a little help
I'll try to struggle on* voice

Spare me the promise and the curse
voice, the ansafoney *Call me, please
when you get in* voice, the *nobody knows
the trouble I've seen* voice; the *I'd value
your advice* voice.

I want the how it was voice;
the *call me irresponsible but aren't I nice* voice;
the *such a bastard but I warn them in advance* voice.
The *We all have weaknesses
and mine is being wicked* voice

the *life's short and wasting time's
the only vice* voice, the *stay in touch,
but out of reach* voice. I want to hear
the *things it's better not to broach* voice
the *things it's wiser not to voice* voice.

*At the end of a love affair, self-pity is to be avoided at all costs. Far better to walk away
with a defiant swagger, pretending that you never really cared in the first place. And
answering machines, voice mail, any place you can leave a message you will later regret,
are to be avoided for at least six months.*

They flee from me, that sometime did me seek
Thomas Wyatt

They flee from me, that sometime did me seek
With naked foot stalking in my chamber.
I have seen them gentle, tame, and meek
That now are wild, and do not remember
That sometime they put themselves in danger
To take bread at my hand; and now they range.
Busily seeking with a continual change.

Thanked be fortune it hath been otherwise
Twenty times better, but once in special.
In thin array after a pleasant guise
When her loose gown from her shoulders did fall,
And she me caught in her arms long and small,
Therewithal sweetly did me kiss,
And softly said, 'Dear heart, how like you this?'

It was no dream: I lay broad waking
But all is turned through my gentleness
Into a strange fashion of forsaking,
And I have leave to go of her goodness,
And she also to use newfangleness.
But since that I so kindly am served,
I would fain know what she hath deserved.

This plangently erotic poem of male disappointment in love was written by one of the men who were accused of having an affair with Anne Boleyn. Its note of emotional bewilderment is surprising in a world where men were the seducers. The way that Wyatt describes his mistress as having arms both 'long and small' is a memorable description of a certain kind of female ruthlessness.

The End of Love
Sophie Hannah

The end of love should be a big event.

It should involve the hiring of a hall.
Why the hell not? It happens to us all.
Why should it pass without acknowledgement?

Suits should be dry-cleaned, invitations sent.
Whatever form it takes — a tiff, a brawl —
The end of love should be a big event.
It should involve the hiring of a hall.

Better than the unquestioning descent
Into the trap of silence, than the crawl
From visible to hidden, door to wall.

Get the announcements made, the money spent.
The end of love should be a big event.
It should involve the hiring of a hall.

The young British poet Sophie Hannah chose the Renaissance verse form of the Petrarchan sonnet to encase the poem's central idea that the end of love deserves just as much public recognition as a wedding, 'it should involve the hiring of a hall'. An uncomfortable idea, although according to a recent edition of American Vogue, 'Divorce parties are the new challenge for the modern hostess.'

The Sunlight on the Garden
Louis MacNeice

The sunlight on the garden
Hardens and grows cold,
We cannot cage the minute
Within its nets of gold;
When all is told
We cannot beg for pardon.

Our freedom as free lances
Advances towards its end;
The earth compels, upon it
Sonnets and birds descend;
And soon, my friend,
We shall have no time for dances.

The sky was good for flying
Defying the church bells
And every evil iron
Siren and what it tells:
The earth compels,
We are dying, Egypt, dying

And not expecting pardon,
Hardened in heart anew,
But glad to have sat under
Thunder and rain with you,
And grateful too
For sunlight on the garden.

The subject of this poem is both MacNeice's ex-wife (he wrote the poem on hearing that she was about to remarry) and World War II. MacNeice is writing about the death of his heart and his fear of literal death from the German bombers. But in the end he finds some comfort in his memories, 'the sunlight on the garden'.

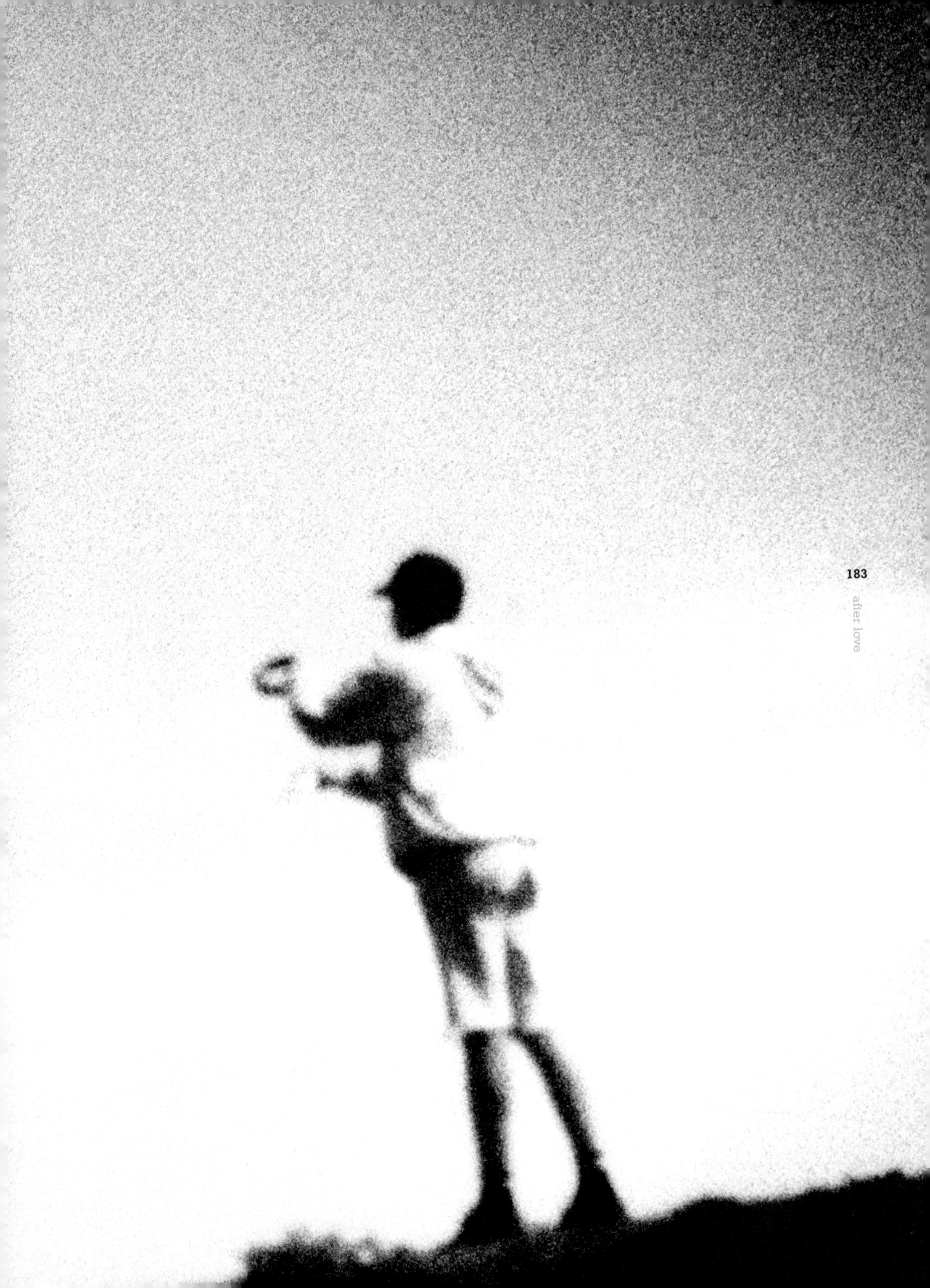

When you are Old
W. B. Yeats

When you are old and grey and full of sleep
And nodding by the fire, take down this book,
And slowly read, and dream of the soft look
Your eyes had once, and of their shadows deep;

How many loved your moments of glad grace,
And loved your beauty with love false or true;
But one man loved the pilgrim soul in you,
And loved the sorrows of your changing face.

And bending down beside the glowing bars,
Murmur, a little sadly, how love fled
And paced upon the mountains overhead,
And hid his face amid a crowd of stars.

after love

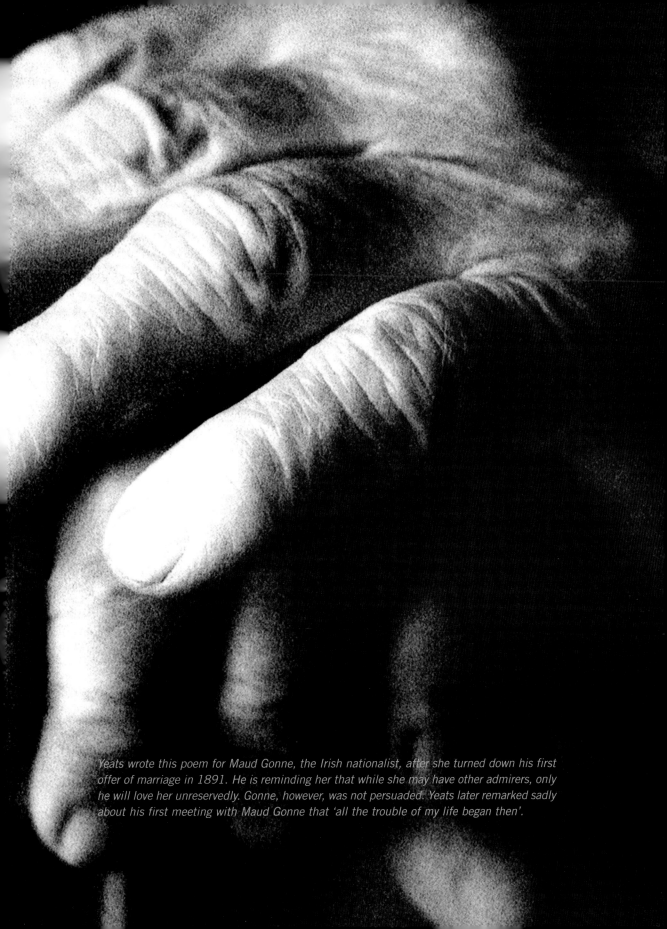

Yeats wrote this poem for Maud Gonne, the Irish nationalist, after she turned down his first offer of marriage in 1891. He is reminding her that while she may have other admirers, only he will love her unreservedly. Gonne, however, was not persuaded. Yeats later remarked sadly about his first meeting with Maud Gonne that 'all the trouble of my life began then'.

I So Liked Spring
Charlotte Mew

I so liked Spring
last year
Because you
were here;–

This poem by Edwardian poet Charlotte Mew is about dealing with the loss of love, when everything, even the seasons, conspires to remind you of your beloved. Contrast the rapturous first five lines with the last bleak quatrain. Mew, a lesbian, was most unlucky in love and committed suicide in 1928 by drinking a bottle of bleach.

The thrushes too –
Because it was these you so liked to hear –
I so liked you.

This year's a different thing –
I'll not think of you.
But I'll like the Spring because it is simply spring
As the thrushes do.

Fire and Ice
Robert Frost

Some say the world will end in fire.
Some say in ice.
From what I've tasted of desire
I hold with those who favor fire.
But if it had to perish twice,
I think I know enough of hate
To say that for destruction ice
Is also great
And would suffice.

Another poem by Robert Frost appears deceptively simple on the surface. I think what Frost is saying here is that there is not much difference between love and hate in their power to destroy what they touch too closely.

Love After Love
Derek Walcott

The time will come
when, with elation,
you will greet yourself arriving
at your own door, in your own mirror,
and each will smile at the other's welcome,

and say, sit here. Eat.
You will love again the stranger who was your self.
Give wine. Give bread. Give back your heart
to itself, to the stranger who has loved you

all your life, whom you ignored
for another, who knows you by heart.
Take down the love letters from the bookshelf,

the photographs, the desperate notes,
peel your own image from the mirror.
Sit. Feast on your life.

This poem by Nobel Prize-winning poet Derek Walcott is a touching injunction to someone after a break-up to learn to love themselves again. How can you expect someone else to love you if you feel completely worthless?

The Thousandth Man
Rudyard Kipling

One man in a thousand, Solomon says,
Will stick more close than a brother.
And it's worth while seeking him half your days
If you find him before the other.
Nine hundred and ninety-nine depend
On what the world sees in you,
But the Thousandth Man will stand your friend
With the whole round world against you.

'Tis neither promise nor prayer nor show
Will settle the finding for 'ee.
Nine hundred and ninety-nine of 'em go
By your looks, or your acts, or your glory.
But if he finds you and you find him,
The rest of the world don't matter;
For the Thousandth Man will sink or swim
With you in any water.

I think we all need the kind of friend that Rudyard Kipling conjures up in this poem.

You can use his purse with no more talk
Than he uses yours for his spendings,
And laugh and meet in your daily walk
As though there had been no lendings.
Nine hundred and ninety-nine of them call
For silver and gold in their dealings;
But the Thousandth Man he's worth 'em all,
Because you can show him your feelings.

His wrong's your wrong, and his right's your right,
In season or out of season.
Stand up and back it in all men's sight –
With that for your only reason!
Nine hundred and ninety-nine can't bide
The shame or mocking or laughter,
But the Thousandth Man will stand by your side
To the gallows-foot – and after!

Not Waving but Drowning
Stevie Smith

Nobody heard him, the dead man,
But still he lay moaning:
I was much further out than you thought
And not waving but drowning.

Poor chap, he always loved larking
And now he's dead
It must have been too cold for him his heart gave way,
They said.

A justly famous poem by Stevie Smith about how easy it is to miss true desparation. A real friend is the one who hears the cry for help.

Oh, no no no, it was too cold always
(Still the dead one lay moaning)
I was much too far out all my life
And not waving but drowning.

A Snarl for Loose Friends
Marge Piercy

Many who say friend,
friend, clutch their balls like prayers
for fear something of themselves
may break loose and get away.

Many who mumble love,
love to keep an eye fixed for the fire
ladder, the exit hatch and at the first
sign of trouble do not hang around to chat.

Many who talk of community
called the real estate agent last night
and the papers are drawn up to sell their land
to a nuclear power plant that shows dirty movies.

Don't count your friends by their buttons
until you have seen them pushed a few times.

A warning about the difference between friends and acquaintances.

The Compassionate Fool
Norman Cameron

My enemy had bidden me as guest.
His table all set out with wine and cake,
His ordered chairs, he to beguile me dressed
So neatly, moved my pity for his sake.

I knew it was an ambush, but could not
Leave him to eat his cake up by himself
And put his unused glasses on the shelf.
I made pretence of falling in his plot,

And trembled when in his anxiety
He bared it too absurdly to my view.
And even as he stabbed me through and through
I pitied him for his small strategy.

This brilliantly subtle poem was recommended to me by a friend when she heard I had been promoted at work. She said it was a reminder that because I was now a boss, I was fair game. 'No one' she said, 'will hesitate to stab you in the back.'

To a Friend Whose Work Has Come To Nothing
W. B. Yeats

Now all the truth is out,
Be secret and take defeat
From any brazen throat,
For how can you compete,
Being honour bred, with one
Who, were it proved he lies,
Were neither shamed in his own
Nor in his neighbours' eyes?
Bred to a harder thing
Than Triumph, turn away
And like a laughing string
Whereon mad fingers play
Amid a place of stone,
Be secret and exult,
Because of all things known
That is most difficult.

This poem is frequently quoted by writers; it seems to have been a touchstone for the anxiety that without an audience for your work, it will never really have existed. The advice to 'be secret and exult' is good, but even Yeats admits it is fiendishly difficult.

If I Can Stop One Heart from Breaking
Emily Dickinson

If I can stop one heart from breaking,
   I shall not live in vain;
If I can ease one life the aching,
   Or cool one pain,
Or help one lonely person
   Into happiness again
I shall not live in vain.

Although Emily Dickinson was a famous recluse, she was always willing to visit people who were sick or had been bereaved. Some of her most memorable poems are about her wish to help her friends or neighbours through hard times.

Still I Rise
Maya Angelou

You may write me down in history
With your bitter, twisted lies,
You may trod me in the very dirt
But still, like dust, I'll rise.

Does my sassiness upset you?
Why are you beset with gloom?
'Cause I walk like I've got oil wells
Pumping in my living room.

Just like the moons and like suns
With the certainty of tides,
Just like hopes springing high,
Still I'll rise.

Did you want to see me broken?
Bowed head and lowered eyes?
Shoulders falling down like teardrops,
Weakened by my soulful cries?

Does my haughtiness offend you?
Don't you take it awful hard
'Cause I laugh like I've got gold mines
Diggin' in my own backyard.

You may shoot me with your words,
You may cut me with your eyes,
You may kill me with your hatefulness,
But still, like air, I'll rise.

Does my sexiness upset you?
Does it come as a surprise
That I dance like I've got diamonds
At the meeting of my thighs?

Out of the huts of history's shame
I rise
Up from a past that's rooted in pain
I rise
I'm a black ocean, leaping and wide,
Welling and swelling I bear in the tide.

Leaving behind nights of terror and fear
I rise
Into a daybreak that's wondrously clear
I rise
Bringing the gifts that my ancestors gave,
I am the dream and the hope of the slave.
I rise
I rise
I rise.

The American writer Maya Angelou has written no less than five volumes of autobiography. She has been, among other things, an actress, a civil-rights activist, novelist, playwright and poet. This poem is her personal manifesto – an expression of her extraordinary zest for life. Famous since its publication, it has been adopted by women everywhere as a personal themesong.

Anthem
Arthur Hugh Clough

themesongs

Say not the struggle nought availeth,
    The labour and the wounds are vain,
The enemy faints not, nor faileth,
    And as things have been, things remain.

If hopes were dupes, fears may be liars;
    It may be, in yon smoke conceal'd,
Your comrades chase e'en now the fliers,
    And, but for you, possess the field.

For while the tired waves, vainly breaking,
    Seem here no painful inch to gain,
Far back through creeks and inlets making
    Came, silent, flooding in, the main,

And not by eastern windows only,
    When daylight comes, comes in the light,
In front the sun climbs slow, how slowly,
    But westward, look, the land is bright.

Just reading this poem by the Victorian poet Arthur Clough makes you want to sit up straighter and stiffen that upper lip. The poem was first published in 1855 and was probably directed at the defeated liberals who had attempted to overthrow the reactionary regimes in France and Italy in 1848.

W. E. Henley

Out of the night that covers me,
   Black as the pit from pole to pole,
I thank whatever gods may be
   For my unconquerable soul.

In the fell clutch of circumstance
   I have not winced nor cried aloud:
Under the bludgeonings of chance
   My head is bloody, but unbowed.

Beyond this place of wrath and tears
   Looms but the Horror of the shade,
And yet the menace of the years
   Finds and shall find me unafraid.

It matters not how strait the gate,
   How charged with punishment the scroll,
I am the master of my fate:
   I am the captain of my soul.

W. E. Henley suffered from a tubercular disease as a child and eventually as a young man had to have his foot amputated (his life was saved by the surgeon Lister). He wrote 'Invictus' (which means unconquerable in Latin) while in hospital recovering from his operation.

As Much as You Can

C.P. Cavafy

(translated from the Greek by Edmund Keeley and Philip Sherrard)

Even if you can't shape your life the way you want,
at least try as much as you can
not to degrade it
by too much contact with the world,
by too much activity and talk.

Do not degrade it by dragging it along,
taking it around and exposing it so often
to the daily silliness
of social relations and parties,
until it comes to seem a boring hanger-on.

203

themesongs

Another poem by the great Cavafy: this one about the importance of living with honour and not letting yourself be seduced from your true purpose by the easy life.

Stopping by Woods on a Snowy Evening
Robert Frost

Whose woods these are I think I know.
His house is in the village, though;
He will not see me stopping here
To watch his woods fill up with snow.

My little horse must think it's queer
To stop without a farmhouse near
Between the woods and frozen lake
The darkest evening of the year.

He gives his harness bells a shake
To ask if there is some mistake.
The only other sound's the sweep
Of easy wind and downy flake.

The woods are lovely, dark, and deep,
But I have promises to keep,
And miles to go before I sleep,
And miles to go before I sleep.

The meaning of this poem has been endlessly debated. Frost himself hated the discussion over the poem's 'true' meaning. For him, the only valid interpretation was the one the reader brought to the poem. My reading of the poem is this: the seductive snowy woods represent the easy way out, but then the horse with its jingling harness bells is the voice in your head which tells you to pull yourself together and find the strength to carry on.

If
Rudyard Kipling

If you can keep your head when all about you
    Are losing theirs and blaming it on you,
If you can trust yourself when all men doubt you,
    But make allowance for their doubting too;
If you can wait and not be tired by waiting,
    Or being lied about, don't deal in lies,
Or being hated, don't give way to hating,
    And yet don't look too good, nor talk too wise:

If you can dream – and not make dreams your master;
    If you can think – and not make thoughts your aim;
If you can meet with Triumph and Disaster
    And treat those two impostors both the same;
If you can bear to hear the truth you've spoken
    Twisted by knaves to make a trap for fools,
Or watch the things you gave your life to, broken,
    And stoop and build 'em up with worn-out tools:

This iconic poem has been much parodied (notably by the Rastafarian poet Benjamin Zephaniah) but whether you agree with its definition of manhood or not, there is no doubt that it is unforgettable. In 1996 it was officially voted the Nation's Favourite Poem by BBC viewers and listeners, receiving more votes than all the other poems put together.

If you can make one heap of all your winnings
    And risk it on one turn of pitch-and-toss,
And lose, and start again at your beginnings
    And never breathe a word about your loss;
If you can force your heart and nerve and sinew
    To serve your turn long after they are gone,
And so hold on when there is nothing in you
    Except the Will which says to them: 'Hold on!'

If you can talk with crowds and keep your virtue,
    Or walk with Kings – nor lose the common touch,
If neither foes nor loving friends can hurt you,
    If all men count with you, but none too much;
If you can fill the unforgiving minute
    With sixty seconds' worth of distance run,
Yours is the Earth and everything that's in it,
    And – which is more – you'll be a Man, my son!

Ships
Maya Angelou

themesongs

Ships?
Sure I'll sail them.
Show me the boat,
If it'll float,
I'll sail it.

Men?
Yes I'll love them.
If they've got the style,
To make me smile,
I'll love them.

Life?
'Course I'll live it.
let me have breath,
Just to my death,
And I'll live it.

Failure?
I'm not ashamed to tell it,
I never learned to spell it.
Not Failure.

Another shout of sassy, full-throated defiance against inadequacy by Maya Angelou.

Happy the Man
Happy the Man
John Dryden

Happy the man, and happy he alone,
    He who can call today his own:
    He who, secure within, can say,
Tomorrow do thy worst, for I have lived today.
    Be fair or foul or rain or shine
The joys I have possessed, in spite of fate, are mine.
Not Heaven itself upon the past has power,
But what has been, has been, and I have had my hour.

This translation from Horace is quite evidently the prescription for a truly happy life.

Musée des Beaux Arts
W. H. Auden

About suffering they were never wrong,
The Old Masters: how well they understood
Its human position; how it takes place
While someone else is eating or opening a window or
   just walking dully along;
How, when the aged are reverently, passionately waiting
For the miraculous birth, there always must be
Children who did not specially want it to happen, skating
On a pond at the edge of the wood:
They never forgot
That even the dreadful martydom must run its course
Anyhow in a corner, some untidy spot
Where the dogs go on with their doggy life and the torturer's horse
Scratches its innocent behind on a tree.

In Brueghel's *Icarus*, for instance: how everything turns away
Quite leisurely from the disaster; the ploughman may
Have heard the splash, the forsaken cry,
But for him it was not an important failure; the sun shone
As it had to on the white legs disappearing into the green
Water; and the expensive delicate ship that must have seen
Something amazing, a boy falling out of the sky,
Had somewhere to get to and sailed calmly on.

211

themesongs

The Leader
Roger McGough

I wanna be the leader
I wanna be the leader
Can I be the leader?
Can I? I can?
Promise? Promise?
Yippee, I'm the leader
I'm the leader

OK what shall we do?

Another poem for children which takes on an adult theme. So many people wish to be the leader in life without really knowing why or how to do it. Roger McGough uses humour to make a serious point about human nature and the lust for power.

Gare du Midi
W. H. Auden

A nondescript express in from the South,
Crowds round the ticket barrier, a face
To welcome which the mayor has not contrived
Bugles or braid: something about the mouth
Distracts the stray look with alarm and pity.
Snow is falling. Clutching a little case,
He walks out briskly to infect a city
Whose terrible future may have just arrived.

A chilling poem written fifty-odd years ago that is once again horribly relevant.

First They Came for the Jews
Pastor Niemöller

First they came for the Jews
and I did not speak out –
because I was not a Jew.
Then they came for the communists
and I did not speak out –
because I was not a communist.
Then they came for the trade unionists
and I did not speak out –
because I was not a trade unionist.
Then they came for me –
and there was no one left
to speak out for me.

Pastor Niemöller was a U-boat commander in World War I. He was ordained as a clergyman in 1924, relieved of his post by the Nazis in 1934 and sent to a concentration camp three years later for publicly opposing the regime. Miraculously, he survived. This poem is an extraordinary record of his struggle with his conscience.

Out There
Michael Longley

Do they ever meet out there,
The dolphins I counted,
The otter I wait for?
I should have spent my life
Listening to the waves.

Think of this poem the next time you find yourself making a commitment you don't have the time or the inclination to honour. In the end, what are the things you will really regret not doing?

Annus Mirabilis
Philip Larkin

Sexual intercourse began
In nineteen sixty-three
(which was rather late for me) –
Between the end of the 'Chatterley' ban
And the Beatles' first LP.

Up to then there'd only been
A sort of bargaining,
A wrangle for the ring,
A shame that started at sixteen
And spread to everything.

Then all at once the quarrel sank:
Everyone felt the same,
And every life became
A brilliant breaking of the bank,
A quite unlosable game.

So life was never better than
In nineteen sixty-three
(Though just too late for me) –
Between the end of the 'Chatterley' ban
And the Beatles' first LP.

Larkin is referring here to the invention of the Pill in 1963. Of course, being Larkin, he has to point out that the sexual revolution has come too late for him, it is everybody else who is having the fun.

To a Fat Lady Seen from the Train
Triolet
Frances Cornford

O why do you walk through the fields in gloves,
  Missing so much and so much?
O fat white woman whom nobody loves,
Why do you walk through the fields in gloves,
When the grass is soft as the breast of doves
  And shivering-sweet to the touch?
O why do you walk through the fields in gloves,
  Missing so much and so much?

A haunting poem about the importance of not protecting yourself so much in life that you never feel the important things.

A Woman of a Certain Age
Carol Rumens

'This must have been my life
but I never lived it.'
– Her childishly wide stare
at some diminishing reel
of space and brightness, half
illusory, half not,
stuns to an epitaph.
And I can read it all:
how a little lie
whitened to twenty years;
how she was chosen by
something called happiness,
yet nothing, nothing was hers.
And now she has to turn
away, and her bruised eyes
are smiling in their nets:
'It's simple, isn't it?
Never say the yes
you don't mean, but the no
you always meant, say that,
even if it's too late,
even if it kills you.'

*A chilling poem about the necessity of courage when making big decisions in your life. Better
that you should learn to say 'No', even if it kills you, rather than the 'Yes' you didn't mean.*

6 a.m. Thoughts
Dick Davis

As soon as you wake they come blundering in
　　Like puppies or importunate children;
What was a landscape emerging from mist
　　Becomes at once a disordered garden.

And the mess they trail with them! Embarrassments,
　　Anger, lust, fear – in fact the whole pig-pen;
And who'll clean it up? No hope for sleep now –
　　Just heave yourself out, make the tea, and give in.

—

This poem is for anyone who has woken up rigid with horror with the memory of what they said or did the night before. As Dick Davis says, the only remedy is to meet your fears head on and make the tea.

Things
Fleur Adcock

There are worse things than having behaved foolishly in public.
There are worse things than these miniature betrayals,
committed or endured or suspected; there are worse things
than not being able to sleep for thinking about them.
It is 5am. All the worse things come stalking in
and stand icily about the bed looking worse and worse and
    worse.

No comfort here, but this poem might make you laugh at the absurdity of small-hour anxieties.

The City
C. P. Cavafy

You said: 'I'll go to another country, go to another shore,
find another city better than this one.
Whatever I try to do is fated to turn out wrong
and my heart – like something dead – lies buried.
How long can I let my mind moulder in this place?
Wherever I turn, wherever I look,
I see the black ruins of my life, here,
where I've spent so many years, wasted them, destroyed them totally.'

Most of us have an 'if-only' fantasy that usually takes place in some parallel sun-baked universe. But, as this rather grim poem points out, you can't escape from yourself. Depressing, but a very good reason not to buy that dodgy time-share.

You won't find a new country, won't find another shore.
This city will always pursue you.
You'll walk the same streets, grow old
in the same neighbourhoods, turn grey in these same houses.
You'll always end up in this city. Don't hope for things elsewhere:
there's no ship for you, there's no road.
Now that you've wasted your life here, in this small corner,
you've destroyed it everywhere in the world.

In praise of feeling bad about yourself
Wislawa Szymborska

The buzzard never says it is to blame.
The panther wouldn't know what scruples mean.
When the piranha strikes, it feels no shame.
If snakes had hands, they'd claim their hands were clean.

A jackal doesn't understand remorse.
Lions and lice don't waver in their course.
Why should they, when they know they're right?

Though hearts of killer whales may weigh a ton,
in every other way they're light.

On this third planet of the sun
among the signs of bestiality
a clear conscience is Number One.

The counselling industry is full of cheery slogans that encourage you to ban remorse and look unflinchingly ahead into the shining future. But, as one who is congenitally guilty, I sympathize with the Polish poet Wislawa Szymborska's argument that a guilty conscience is what makes us human.

Adlestrop
Edward Thomas

Yes, I remember Adlestrop –
The name, because one afternoon
Of heat the express-train drew up there
Unwontedly. It was late June.

The steam hissed. Someone cleared his throat.
No one left and no one came
On the bare platform. What I saw
Was Adlestrop – only the name

And willows, willow-herb, and grass,
And meadowsweet, and haycocks dry,
No whit less still and lonely fair
Than the high cloudlets in the sky.

And for that minute a blackbird sang
Close by, and round him, mistier,
Farther and farther, all the birds
Of Oxfordshire and Gloucestershire.

Edward Thomas started writing poetry in his thirties with the encouragement of his friend Robert Frost. This new medium seemed to unleash his creativity and in the few years left before his death at the end of World War I he produced an astonishing body of work. This poem is about the transforming power of memory – something that Thomas who joined up as a private soldier in 1915, must have relied on while serving on the trenches.

Into my heart an air that kills
A. E. Housman

Into my heart an air that kills
From yon far country blows:
What are those blue remembered hills?
What spires, what farms are those?

memories

This famous passage from *A Shropshire Lad* is both poetically gorgeous and powerfully astute about the lethal glamour of nostalgia.

That is the land of lost content,
 I see it shining plain,
The happy highways where I went
 And cannot come again.

I remember, I remember
Thomas Hood

I remember, I remember,
The house where I was born,
The little window where the sun
Came peeping in at morn;
He never came a wink too soon,
Nor brought too long a day,
But now, I often wish the night
Had borne my breath away!

I remember, I remember,
The roses, red and white,
The violets, and the lily-cups,
Those flowers made of light!
The lilacs where the robin built,
And where my brother set
The laburnum on his birthday, -
The tree is living yet!

I remember, I remember,
Where I was used to swing,
And thought the air must rush as fresh
To swallows on the wing;
My spirit flew in feathers then,
That is so heavy now,
And summer pools could hardly cool
The fever on my brow!

I remember, I remember,
The fir trees dark and high;
I used to think their slender tops
Were close against the sky:
It was a childish ignorance,
But now 'tis little joy
To know I'm farther off from heav'n
Than when I was a boy.

I remember my childhood as something I am quite glad to have left behind; but for poets there is something irresistible about the contrast between the innocence of youth and the weight of adult experience. This tremendous poem by the Victorian Thomas Hood is one of the best on this theme I have come across and so inspired Philip Larkin that he wrote a poem using the same title.

That time of year thou mayst in me behold
William Shakespeare

That time of year thou mayst in me behold
When yellow leaves, or none, or few, do hang
Upon those boughs which shake against the cold,
Bare ruin'd choirs, where late the sweet birds sang.
In me thou see'st the twilight of such day
As after sunset fadeth in the west;
Which by and by black night doth take away,
Death's second self, that seals up all in rest.
In me thou see'st the glowing of such fire,
That on the ashes of his youth doth lie,
As the death-bed whereon it must expire
Consum'd with that which it was nourish'd by.
     This thou perceiv'st, which makes thy love more strong,
     To love that well which thou must leave ere long.

To most of us, getting older is something that we resign ourselves to, but to poets the ageing process is a treasure trove of new subject matter. Shakespeare wrote one of his greatest sonnets on the subject of growing old.

On His Baldness

Po Chü-I

(translated from the Chinese by Arthur Waley)

At dawn I sighed to see my hairs fall;
At dusk I sighed to see my hairs fall.
For I dreaded the time when the last lock should go . . .
They are all gone and I do not mind at all!
I have done with that cumbrous washing and getting dry;
My tiresome comb for ever is laid aside.
Best of all, when the weather is hot and wet,
To have no top-knot weighing down on one's head!
I put aside my messy cloth wrap;
I have got rid of my dusty tasselled fringe.
In a silver jar I have stored a cold stream,
On my bald pate I trickle a ladle full.
Like one baptized with the Water of Buddha's Law,
I sit and receive this cool, cleansing joy.
Now I know why the priest who seeks Repose
Frees his heart by first shaving his head.

Po Chü-I was an eighth-century Chinese poet writing during the Tang dynasty. I have included this poem as a consolation for any man mourning the loss of his topknot. Of course, the poet is making a more serious note about the cumbersome nature of worldly vanity: in his eyes baldness is not a loss but a liberation.

Wishes of an elderly man
Sir Walter Raleigh

I wish I loved the Human Race;
I wish I loved its silly face;
I wish I liked the way it walks;
I wish I liked the way it talks;
And when I'm introduced to one
I wish I thought *What Jolly Fun!*

The Chinese are clearly better at growing old gracefully than the British. Here is the classic Grumpy Old Man poem from an Edwardian, Sir Walter Raleigh, a decidedly ungallant descendant of the man with the cloak.

Senex
John Betjeman

Oh would I could subdue the flesh
Which sadly troubles me!
And then perhaps could view the flesh
As though I never knew the flesh
And merry misery.

To see the golden hiking girl
With wind about her hair,
The tennis-playing, biking girl,
The wholly-to-my-liking girl,
To see and not to care.

At sundown on my tricycle
I tour the Borough's edge,
And icy as an icicle
See bicycle by bicycle
Stacked waiting in the hedge.

Get down from me! I thunder there,
You spaniels! Shut your jaws!
Your teeth are stuffed with underwear,
Suspenders torn asunder there
And buttocks in your paws!

Oh whip the dogs away my Lord,
They make me ill with lust.
Bend bare knees down to pray, my Lord,
Teach sulky lips to say, my Lord,
That flaxen hair is dust.

*Only John Betjeman could write with such disarming candour about the inappropriateness
of lusting after firmer flesh in your bus-pass years.*

Mirror
Sylvia Plath

getting older

I am silver and exact. I have no preconceptions.
Whatever I see I swallow immediately
Just as it is, unmisted by love or dislike.
I am not cruel, only truthful –
The eye of a little god, four-cornered.
Most of the time I meditate on the opposite wall.
It is pink, with speckles. I have looked at it so long
I think it is a part of my heart. But it flickers.
Faces and darkness separate us over and over.

Now I am a lake. A woman bends over me,
Searching my reaches for what she really is.
Then she turns to those liars, the candles or the moon,
I see her back, and reflect it faithfully.
She rewards me with tears and an agitation of hands.
I am important to her. She comes and goes.
Each morning it is her face that replaces the darkness.
In me she has drowned a young girl, and in me an old woman
Rises toward her day after day, like a terrible fish.

I once spent three months living in the Amazon jungle. Among the many things I did not have was a mirror. This was strangely liberating; I hadn't realised until that point quite how much time I spent thinking about my appearance. Now I avoid mirrors as I avoid bathroom scales, ignorance is bliss. This chilling poem by Sylvia Plath is worse than any mirror.

The Old Familiar Faces
Charles Lamb

I HAVE had playmates, I have had companions,
In my days of childhood, in my joyful school-days:
All, all are gone, the old familiar faces.

I have been laughing, I have been carousing,
Drinking late, sitting late, with my bosom cronies:
All, all are gone, the old familiar faces.

I loved a Love once, fairest among women:
Closed are her doors on me, I must not see her –
All, all are gone, the old familiar faces.

I have a friend, a kinder friend has no man:
Like an ingrate, I left my friend abruptly;
Left him, to muse on the old familiar faces.

Ghost-like I paced round the haunts of my childhood,
Earth seem'd a desert I was bound to traverse,
Seeking to find the old familiar faces.

Friend of my bosom, thou more than a brother,
Why wert not thou born in my father's dwelling?
So might we talk of the old familiar faces-

How some they have died, and some they have left me,
And some are taken from me; all are departed-
All, all are gone, the old familiar faces.

A haunting poem about loss and loneliness from Charles Lamb, who was a friend of Shelley, Byron and Coleridge. Lamb's family suffered from mental illness: he had a breakdown at the age of twenty and his sister, a schizophrenic, murdered their mother. This may account for the mood of desolation in the poem.

Getting Older
Elaine Feinstein

The first surprise: I like it.
Whatever happens now, some things
that used to terrify have not:

I didn't die young, for instance. Or lose
my only love. My three children
never had to run away from anyone.

Don't tell me this gratitude is complacent.
We all approach the edge of the same blackness
which for me is silent.

Knowing as much sharpens
my delight in January freesia,
hot coffee, winter sunlight. So we say

as we lie close on some gentle occasion:
every day won from such
darkness is a celebration.

Here are some refreshingly positive thoughts on the subject of ageing. It doesn't hurt sometimes to count your blessings as well as your crow's feet.

Wisdom
Sara Teasdale

When I have ceased to break my wings
Against the faultiness of things,
And learned that compromises wait
Behind each hardly opened gate,
When I can look Life in the eyes,
Grown calm and very coldly wise,
Life will have given me the Truth,
And taken in exchange – my youth.

Sara Teasdale was one of the most successful poets in America at the beginning of the twentieth century (winning the first Pulitzer prize for poetry) but she has since gone out of fashion. I am a fan of her simple lyrical poems, like this one about the downside of learning from experience.

Tell me now
Wang Chi
(translated from the Chinese by Arthur Waley)

'Tell me now, what should a man want
But to sit alone, sipping his cup of wine?'
I should like to have visitors come and discuss philosophy
And not to have the tax-collector coming to collect taxes;
My three sons married into good families
And my five daughters wedded to steady husbands.
Then I could jog through a happy five-score years
And, at the end, need no Paradise.

I like this fifth-century Chinese prescription for a contented (and extended) old age.

Madam Life's a piece in bloom
W. E. Henley

Madam Life's a piece in bloom
  Death goes dogging everywhere:
She's the tenant of the room,
  He's the ruffian on the stair.

You shall see her as a friend,
  You shall bilk him once and twice;
But he'll trap you in the end,
  And he'll stick you for her price.

With his kneebones at your chest,
  And his knuckles in your throat,
You would reason – plead – protest!
  Clutching at her petticoat;

But she's heard it all before,
  Well she knows you've had your fun,
Gingerly she gains the door,
  And your little job is done.

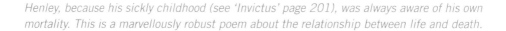

Henley, because his sickly childhood (see 'Invictus' page 201), was always aware of his own mortality. This is a marvellously robust poem about the relationship between life and death.

Every Morning
Alice Walker

Every morning I exercise
my body.
It complains
'Why are you doing this to me?'
I give it a plié
in response.
I heave my legs
off the floor
and feel my stomach muscles
rebel:
they are mutinous
there are rumblings
of dissent.
I have other things
to show,
but mostly, my body.

'Don't you see that person
staring at you?' I ask my breasts,
which are still capable
of staring back.
'If I didn't exercise
you couldn't look up
that far.
Your life would be nothing
but shoes.'
'Let us at least say we're doing it
for ourselves';
my fingers are eloquent;
they never sweat.

I have recently discovered, to my sorrow, that 'love handles' are more than a figure of speech. I have therefore included this poem as a reminder (as if we needed one!) of the importance of defying gravity. As the poet says ruefully, 'I have other things / to show, / but mostly, my body.'

What Fifty Said
Robert Frost

When I was young my teachers were the old.
I gave up fire for form till I was cold.
I suffered like a metal being cast.
I went to school to age to learn the past.

Now I am old my teachers are the young.
What can't be molded must be cracked and sprung.
I strain at lessons fit to start a suture.
I go to school to youth to learn the future.

A poem that illustrates Frost's essential humility. One might have thought that someone who had reached Frost's level of fame and . . . success might feel they had nothing more to learn, but Frost is willing to 'go to school to learn the future'. If only more fifty-year old politicians would say the same!

Warning
Jenny Joseph

When I am an old woman I shall wear purple
With a red hat which doesn't go, and doesn't suit me.
And I shall spend my pension on brandy and summer gloves
And satin sandals, and say we've no money for butter.
I shall sit down on the pavement when I'm tired
And gobble up samples in shops and press alarm bells
And run my stick along the public railings
And make up for the sobriety of my youth.
I shall go out in my slippers in the rain
And pick the flowers in other people's gardens
And learn to spit.

You can wear terrible shirts and grow more fat
And eat three pounds of sausages at a go
Or only bread and pickle for a week
And hoard pens and pencils and beermats and things in boxes.

But now we must have clothes that keep us dry
And pay our rent and not swear in the street
And set a good example for the children.
We must have friends to dinner and read the papers.

But maybe I ought to practise a little now?
So people who know me are not too shocked and surprised
When suddenly I am old, and start to wear purple.

getting older

This poem about growing old disgracefully was recently voted the Nation's Favourite twentieth-century poem, much to its author Jenny Joseph's chagrin (she feels the success of this poem has overshadowed other, better work). But I make no apologies for including it here: I look forward to becoming unrepentantly eccentric in my senior years.

Kissing
Fleur Adcock

The young are walking on the riverbank,
arms around each other's waists and shoulders,
pretending to be looking at the waterlilies
and what might be a nest of some kind, over
there, which two who are clamped together
mouth to mouth have forgotten about.
The others, making courteous detours
around them, talk, stop talking, kiss.
They can see no one older than themselves.
It's their river. They've got all day.

Seeing's not everything. At this very
moment the middle-aged are kissing
in the backs of taxis, on the way
to airports and stations. Their mouths and tongues
are soft and powerful and as moist as ever.
Their hands are not inside each other's clothes
(because of the driver) but locked so tightly
together that it hurts: it may leave marks
on their not of course youthful skin, which they won't
notice. They too may have futures.

When you are young there is nothing more depressing than the thought of middle-aged canoodling, but as you get older it is hugely cheering to find that some things actually improve with age.

So we'll go no more a-roving
Lord Byron

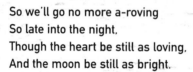

getting older

So we'll go no more a-roving
So late into the night,
Though the heart be still as loving,
And the moon be still as bright.

For the sword outwears its sheath,
And the soul wears out the breast,
And the heart must pause to breathe,
And Love itself have rest.

Though the night was made for loving,
And the day returns too soon,
Yet we'll go no more a-roving
By the light of the moon.

Byron dashed off this poem one night in Venice, a city where he claimed to have slept with two hundred women in two years. No wonder his 'sword' had outworn its 'sheath' – the poet was in a state of complete sexual exhaustion. But at twenty-nine Byron recovered quickly and within days of writing this poem, he was back in his gondola looking for his next conquest.

Scintillate
Roger McGough

I have outlived
my youthfulness
so a quiet life for me

where once
I used to
scintillate

now I sin
till ten
past three.

Let's hope we are all able to sin till late like Roger McGough.

A Song of a Young Lady to Her Ancient Lover
John Wilmot, Earl of Rochester

Ancient person, for whom I
All the flattering youth defy,
Long be it ere thou grow old,
Aching, shaking, crazy, cold;
   But still continue as thou art,
   Ancient person of my heart.

On thy withered lips and dry,
Which like barren furrows lie,
Brooding kisses I will pour
Shall thy youthful heat restore
(Such kind showers in autumn fall,
And a second spring recall);
   Nor from thee will ever part,
   Ancient person of my heart.

Thy nobler part, which but to name
In our sex would be counted shame,
By age's frozen grasp possessed,
From his ice shall be released,
And soothed by my reviving hand
In former warmth and vigor stand.
All a lover's wish can reach
For thy joy my love shall teach,
And for thy pleasure shall improve
All that art can add to love.
   Yet still I love thee without art,
   Ancient person of my heart.

Rochester, the Restoration poet who gave Byron a run for his money when it comes to disreputable behaviour, here writes about every older man's fantasy. Imagine this poem issuing from the lips of Anna Nicole Smith.

Mr Teodoro Luna's two kisses
Alberto Rios

Mr Teodoro Luna in his later years had taken to kissing
His wife
Not so much with his lips as with his brows.
This is not to say he put his forehead
Against her mouth –
Rather, he would lift his eyebrows, once, quickly:
Not so vigorously he might be confused with the villain
Famous in the theaters, but not so little as to be thought
A slight movement, one of accident. This way
He kissed her
Often and quietly, across tables and through doorways,
Sometimes in photographs, and so through the years themselves.
This was his passion, that only she might see. The chance
He might feel some movement on her lips
Toward laughter.

The Mexican poet Alberto Rios was inspired to write this tender poem by the relationship between his grandparents. It is a superb description of the force-field of non-verbal communication that exists between the truly well matched.

A Joy to Be Old
Roger McGough

It's a joy to be old.
Kids through school,
The dog dead and the car sold.

Worth their weight in gold.
Bus passes. Let asses rule.
It's a joy to be old.

The library when it's cold.
Immune from ridicule.
The dog dead and the car sold.

Time now to be bold.
Skinnydipping in the pool.
It's a joy to be old.

Death cannot be cajoled.
No rewinding the spool.
The dog dead and the car sold.

Get out and get arse'oled.
Have fun playing the fool.
It's a joy to be old.
The dog dead and the car sold.

In America, it is not uncommon to be overtaken on the freeway by massive mobile homes with bumper stickers proclaiming 'We're spending the children's inheritance'. I think a second childhood has much to be said for it.

Funeral Blues
W. H. Auden

Stop all the clocks, cut off the telephone,
Prevent the dog from barking with a juicy bone,
Silence the pianos and with muffled drum
Bring out the coffin, let the mourners come.

Let aeroplanes circle moaning overhead
Scribbling on the sky the message He Is Dead,
Put crepe bows round the white necks of the public doves,
Let the traffic policemen wear black cotton gloves.

He was my North, my South, my East and West,
My working week and my Sunday rest,
My noon, my midnight, my talk, my song;
I thought that love would last for ever; I was wrong.

The stars are not wanted now: put out every one;
Pack up the moon and dismantle the sun;
Pour away the ocean and sweep up the wood,
For nothing now can ever come to any good.

'Funeral Blues' is another example of a poem which has taken on a life of its own. It was originally written in 1936 as a satire on the extravagant expressions of grief that attended the death of dictators. Sky-writing planes were the sort of thing that marked the funeral of a lost leader, not a lost lover. The poem lay dormant until John Hannah read it so memorably at the funeral in the film Four Weddings and a Funeral. *Since then, it has entered the national psyche as THE poem of bereavement.*

The Voice
Thomas Hardy

Woman much missed, how you call to me, call to me,
Saying that now you are not as you were
When you had changed from the one who was all to me,
But as at first, when our day was fair.

Can it be you that I hear? Let me view you, then,
Standing as when I drew near to the town
Where you would wait for me: yes, as I knew you then,
Even to the original air-blue gown!

Or is it only the breeze, in its listlessness
Travelling across the wet mead to me here,
You being ever dissolved to wan wistlessness,
heard no more again far or near?

　　Thus I; faltering forward,
　　Leaves around me falling,
Wind oozing thin through the thorn from norward,
　　And the woman calling.

Thomas Hardy's marriage to Emma Gifford was famously unhappy. He even designed their house near Dorchester so that there was no indoor route between her room and his. But after her death in 1912, Hardy was overcome with grief (guilt?) and wrote some of his best poems mourning the loss of the woman he had treated so badly.

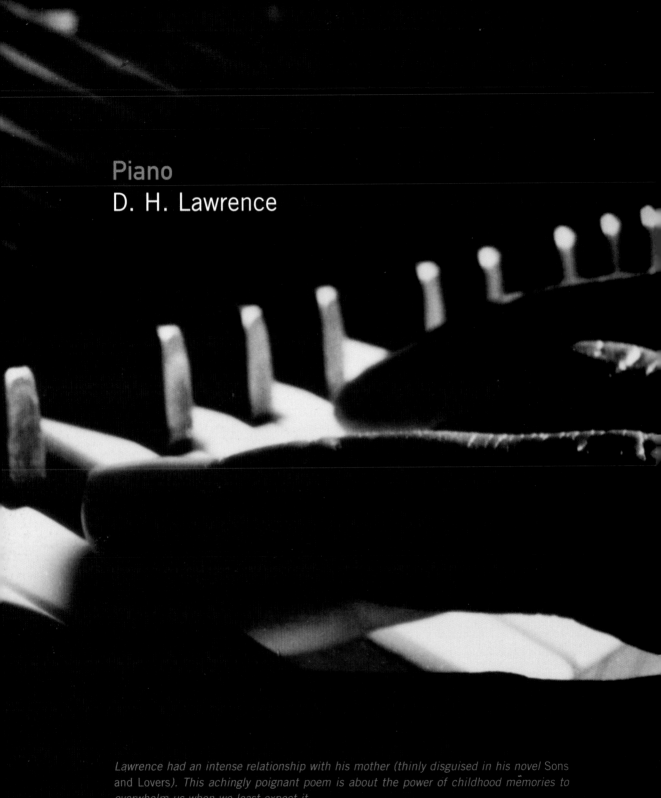

Piano

D. H. Lawrence

Lawrence had an intense relationship with his mother (thinly disguised in his novel Sons and Lovers*). This achingly poignant poem is about the power of childhood memories to overwhelm us when we least expect it.*

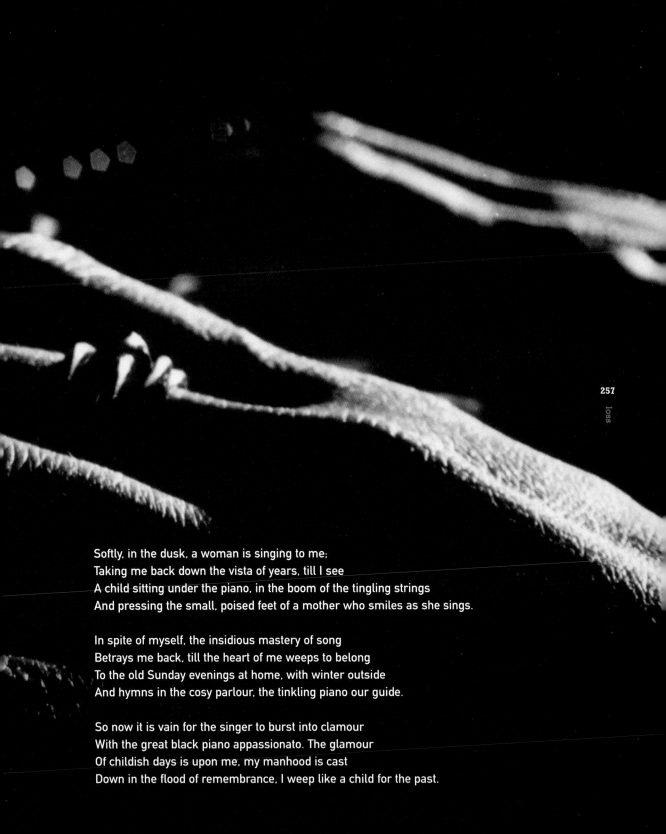

Softly, in the dusk, a woman is singing to me;
Taking me back down the vista of years, till I see
A child sitting under the piano, in the boom of the tingling strings
And pressing the small, poised feet of a mother who smiles as she sings.

In spite of myself, the insidious mastery of song
Betrays me back, till the heart of me weeps to belong
To the old Sunday evenings at home, with winter outside
And hymns in the cosy parlour, the tinkling piano our guide.

So now it is vain for the singer to burst into clamour
With the great black piano appassionato. The glamour
Of childish days is upon me, my manhood is cast
Down in the flood of remembrance, I weep like a child for the past.

A Slumber Did My Spirit Seal
William Wordsworth

A slumber did my spirit seal;
   I had no human fears:
She seemed a thing that could not feel
   The touch of earthly years.

No motion has she now, no force:
   She neither hears nor sees;
Rolled round in earth's diurnal course,
   With rocks, and stones, and trees.

Wordsworth is trying to temper his grief with the thought that death is part of the natural order of things.

Western wind, when will thou blow
Anon.

Western wind, when will thou blow
The small rain down can rain?
Christ, if my love were in my arms
And I in my bed again!

A classic howl of desolation from Anon.

From Childe Harold's Pilgrimage
Lord Byron

They mourn, but smile at length: and, smiling, mourn:
The tree will wither long before it fall:
The hull drives on, though mast and sail be torn:
The roof-tree sinks, but moulders on the hall
In massy hoariness; the ruined wall
Stands when its wind-worn battlements are gone:
The bars survive the captive they enthrall.
The day drags through; storms keep out the sun;
And thus the heart will break, yet brokenly live on.

Byron may have cultivated the image of being 'mad, bad and dangerous to know', but he was hugely sensitive to suffering. Here, he is writing with great compassion about the power of the human spirit to survive tragedy. What Byron is saying is that yes, the agony will pass, but no, you won't ever be the same again.

Break, Break, Break
Alfred Lord Tennyson

Break, break, break,
   On thy cold gray stones, O sea!
And I would that my tongue could utter
   The thoughts that arise in me.

O, well for the fisherman's boy,
   That he shouts with his sister at play!
O, well for the sailor lad,
   That he sings in his boat on the bay!

And the stately ships go on
   To their haven under the hill;
But O for the touch of a vanished hand,
   And the sound of a voice that is still!

Break, break, break,
   At the foot of thy crags, O sea!
But the tender grace of a day that is dead
   Will never come back to me.

These lines are from In Memoriam, *Tennyson's verse lament for his friend Arthur Hallam.*
They present an extraordinarily desolate soundscape of grief.

One Art
Elizabeth Bishop

The art of losing isn't hard to master;
so many things seem filled with the intent
to be lost that their loss is no disaster.

Lose something every day. Accept the fluster
of lost door keys, the hour badly spent.
The art of losing isn't hard to master.

Then practice losing farther, losing faster:
places, and names, and where it was you meant
to travel. None of these will bring disaster.

I lost my mother's watch. And look! my last, or
next-to-last, of three loved houses went.
The art of losing isn't hard to master.

I lost two cities, lovely ones. And, vaster,
some realms I owned, two rivers, a continent.
I miss them, but it wasn't a disaster.

— Even losing you (the joking voice, a gesture
I love) I shan't have lied. It's evident
the art of losing's not too hard to master
though it may look like (*Write* it!) like disaster.

The heart of this poem is an ironic attempt to come to terms with loss by pretending it is a skill which can be mastered. Bishop wrote it in 1975 at a time when she was drinking too much and on the verge of splitting up with her young lover Alice Methfessel. The poem went through seventeen drafts until Bishop was satisfied. I think it is an extraordinary poem about trying (and failing) to laugh in the face of loss.

Sorrow
D. H. Lawrence

Why does the thin grey strand
Floating up from the forgotten
Cigarette between my fingers,
Why does it trouble me?

Ah, you will understand;
When I carried my mother downstairs,
A few times only, at the beginning
Of her soft-foot malady,

I should find, for a reprimand
to my gaiety, a few long grey hairs
On the breast of my coat; and one by one
I watched them float up the dark chimney.

Lawrence's mother died very slowly from cancer. In the end she was in so much pain that she begged her son to help her die, which he did by giving her a sleeping draught (a scene described in Sons and Lovers*). Like 'Piano' (page 256–7) this poem refers to the stealthy way in which grief can surprise us at random.*

Home is so Sad
Philip Larkin

Home is so sad. It stays as it was left,
Shaped to the comfort of the last to go
As if to win them back. Instead, bereft
Of anyone to please, it withers so,
Having no heart to put aside the theft

And turn again to what it started as,
A joyous shot at how things ought to be,
Long fallen wide. You can see how it was:
Look at the pictures and the cutlery.
The music in the piano stool. That vase.

Larkin, as so often, making something ineffably moving out of the sad realities of life. I always think of this poem when I pass those shops that 'undertake clearances' bursting with the now meaningless details of someone else's existence.

Remember
Christina Rossetti

Remember me when I am gone away,
 Gone far away into the silent land;
 When you can no more hold me by the hand,
Nor I half turn to go yet turning stay.
Remember me when no more day by day,
 You tell me of our future that you planned:
 Only remember me; you understand
It will be late to counsel then or pray.
Yet if you should forget me for a while
 And afterwards remember, do not grieve:
 For if the darkness and corruption leave
 A vestige of the thoughts that once I had,
Better by far you should forget and smile
 Than that you should remember and be sad.

Christina Rossetti was the sister of the poet and painter Dante Gabriel Rossetti and a member of the same Pre-Raphaelite circle. This, probably her most famous poem, makes the unselfish point that she would rather be forgotten than have people be sad, remembering her.

Handbag
Ruth Fainlight

My mother's old leather handbag,
crowded with letters she carried
all through the war. The smell
of my mother's handbag: mints
and lipstick and Coty powder.
The look of those letters, softened
and worn at the edges, opened,
read, and refolded so often.
Letters from my father. Odour
of leather and powder, which ever
since then has meant womanliness,
and love, and anguish, and war.

A vividly evocative poem about the way a whole lifetime can be compressed into a simple object.

Joys That Sting
C. S. Lewis

The poem itself is undated, but it is fairly certain that Lewis (the author of the Narnia books) wrote it as he watched his beloved wife Joy fight the cancer that eventually killed her. The title is both a pun on his wife's name and a bitter reminder of the fact that when you lose someone it is the joys you shared together that later hurt the most, by reminding you of happier times.

'Oh doe not die,' says Donne, 'for I shall hate
All women so.' How false the sentence rings.
Women? But in a life made desolate
It is the joys once shared that have the stings.

To take the old walks alone, or not at all,
To order one pint where I ordered two,
To think of, and then not to make, the small
Time-honoured joke (senseless to all but you);

To laugh (oh, one'll laugh), to talking upon
Themes that we talked upon when you were there,
To make some poor pretence of going on,
Be kind to one's old friends, and seem to care.

While no one (O God) through the years will say
The simplest, common word in just your way.

From **In Memoriam VII**
Alfred Lord Tennyson

Dark house, by which once more I stand
Here in the long unlovely street,
Doors, where my heart was used to beat
So quickly, waiting for a hand,

A hand that can be clasped no more –
Behold me, for I cannot sleep,
And like a guilty thing I creep
At earliest morning to the door.

He is not here; but far away
The noise of life begins again
And ghastly through the drizzling rain
On the bald street breaks the blank day.

Another extract from In Memoriam: *here, Tennyson is writing about the obsessive nature of grief, how it compels him to visit the very places that will give him most pain.*

After great pain, a formal feeling comes
Emily Dickinson

After great pain, a formal feeling comes –
The Nerves sit ceremonious, like Tombs –
The stiff Heart questions was it He, that bore,
And Yesterday, or Centuries before?

The Feet, mechanical, go round –
Of Ground, or Air, or Ought –
A Wooden way
Regardless grown,
A Quartz contentment, like a stone –

This is the Hour of Lead –
Remembered, if outlived,
As Freezing persons, recollect the Snow –
First – Chill – then Stupor – then the letting go –

Anyone who has experienced deep unhappiness will recognise the state of numbness that Dickinson is describing here. This is the point where everything seems hopeless – 'the Hour of Lead'. For an antidote to this poem, read Dickinson's 'Hope is the thing with feathers' (page 105), this moment will pass.

From **Long Distance**

Tony Harrison

Though my mother was already two years dead
Dad kept her slippers warming by the gas,
put hot water bottles her side of the bed
and still went to renew her transport pass.

You couldn't just drop in. You had to phone.
He'd put you off an hour to give him time
to clear away her things and look alone
as though his still raw love were such a crime.

He couldn't risk my blight of disbelief
though sure that very soon he'd hear her key
scrape in the rusted lock and end his grief.
He *knew* she'd just popped out to get the tea.

I believe life ends with death, and that is all.
You haven't both gone shopping; just the same,
in my new black leather phone book there's your name
and the disconnected number I still call.

I was lucky enough to hear Tony Harrison reading this poem. Listening to these lines recited in Harrison's sonorous voice with its flat Yorkshire vowels, I found myself crying for Harrison Senior's delusions. Read this poem aloud and feel it grip your emotions.

Time does not bring relief
Edna St Vincent Millay

loss

Time does not bring relief; you all have lied
Who told me time would ease me of my pain!
I miss him in the weeping of the rain;
I want him at the shrinking of the tide;
The old snows melt from every mountain-side,
And last year's leaves are smoke in every lane;
But last year's bitter loving must remain
Heaped on my heart, and my old thoughts abide!
There are a hundred places where I fear
To go, – so with his memory they brim!
And entering with relief some quiet place
Where never fell his foot or shone his face
I say, 'There is no memory of him here!'
And so stand stricken, so remembering him!

Time is, of course, a great healer; but when one's grief is still raw, to be told this by well-meaning friends brings no comfort. This poem is horribly accurate about the tricks that loss plays on the mind: at the end of the poem the narrator has gone to a spot that she never visited with her lover, only to find that the fact he has no connection with this place makes her miss him even more. This is the poem to read when other people's attempts to

Going Without Saying
(In memory of Joe Flynn)
Bernard O'Donoghue

It is a great pity we don't know
When the dead are going to die.
So that, over a last companionable
Drink, we could tell them
How much we liked them.

Happy the man who, dying, can
Place his hand on his heart and say:
'At least I didn't neglect to tell
The thrush how beautifully she sings.'

*A friend of mine died recently after a long struggle with anorexia. We had been great friends
at school but had drifted apart as adults. But she called me a few weeks before her death
and to my shame I never got round to calling her back. Reading this poem reminded me how
important it is for your own peace of mind to cherish the things that really matter.*

The House
Mary Oliver

Because we lived our several lives
Caught up within the spells of love,
Because we always had to run
Through the enormous yards of day
To do all that we hoped to do,
We did not hear, beneath our lives,
The old walls falling out of true,
Foundations shifting in the dark.
When seedlings blossomed in the eaves,
When branches scratched upon the door
And rain came splashing through the halls,
We made our minor, brief repairs,
And sang upon the crumbling stairs
And danced upon the sodden floors.
For years we lived at peace, until
The rooms themselves began to blend
With time, and empty one by one,
At which we knew, with muted hearts,
That nothing further could be done,
And so rose up, and went away,
Inheritors of breath and love,
Bound to that final black estate
No child can mend or trade away.

Another poem about the importance of attempting, at least, to live each day as if it were your last.

Résumé

Dorothy Parker

Razors pain you;
Rivers are damp;
Acids stain you;
And drugs cause cramp.
Guns aren't lawful;
Nooses give;
Gas smells awful;
You might as well live.

I have included this sardonically humorous poem among these poems about loss and grief because sometimes laughter is the best antidote to despair. Dorothy Parker toyed with the idea of suicide for most of her life, but died naturally in the end. As she says, suicide was just too much trouble.

Cowards
from Julius Caesar, Act II, scene ii
William Shakespeare

Cowards die many times before their deaths:
The valiant never taste of death but once.
Of all the wonders that I yet have heard,
It seems to me most strange that men should fear;
Seeing that death, a necessary end,
Will come, when it will come.

As so often, Shakespeare said it best. Here is Julius Caesar explaining why it is pointless to be afraid of death.

Rain
Edward Thomas

Rain, midnight rain, nothing but the wild rain
On this bleak hut, and solitude, and me
Remembering again that I shall die
And neither hear the rain nor give it thanks
For washing me cleaner than I have been
Since I was born into this solitude.
Blessed are the dead that the rain rains upon:
But here I pray that none whom once I loved
Is dying tonight or lying still awake
Solitary, listening to the rain,
Either in pain or thus in sympathy
Helpless among the living and the dead,
Like a cold water among broken reeds,
Myriads of broken reeds all still and stiff,
Like me who have no love which this wild rain
Has not dissolved except the love of death,
If love it be forwards what is perfect and
Cannot, the tempest, tells me, disappoint.

Thomas wrote this in France in January 1916 while he was being trained for active service. The hut he refers to is an army hut. The poem is clearly an attempt to reconcile himself to the end that almost certainly awaited him in the trenches. Thomas was killed by a shell explosion on 9th April 1917, just as the Arras offensive began.

When I have fears that I may cease to be

John Keats

When I have fears that I may cease to be
Before my pen has glean'd my teeming brain,
Before high-piled books, in charactery,
Hold like rich garners the full-ripen'd grain;
When I behold, upon the night's starr'd face,
Huge cloudy symbols of a high romance,
And think that I may never live to trace
Their shadows, with the magic hand of chance;
And when I feel, fair creature of an hour!
That I shall never look upon thee more,
Never have relish in the faery power
Of unreflecting love; – then on the shore
   Of the wide world I stand alone, and think,
   Till love and fame to nothingness do sink.

Wants
Philip Larkin

Beyond all this, the wish to be alone:
However the sky grows dark with invitation-cards
However we follow the printed directions of sex
However the family is photographed under the flagstaff –
Beyond all this, the wish to be alone.

Beneath it all, desire of oblivion runs:
Despite the artful tensions of the calendar,
The life insurance, the tabled fertility rites,
The costly aversion of the eyes from death –
Beneath it all, desire of oblivion runs.

Philip Larkin at his most magnificiently gloomy.

Memento Mori
Billy Collins

There is no need for me to keep a skull on my desk,
to stand with one foot up on the ruins of Rome
or wear a locket with the sliver of a saint's bone

It is enough to realise that every common object
in this sunny little room will outlive me –
the carpet, radio, bookstand and rocker

Not one of these things will attend my burial
not even this dented gooseneck lamp
with its steady benediction of light,

though I could put worse things in my mind
than the image of it waddling across the cemetery
like an old servant, dragging the trail of its cord,
the small circle of mourners parting to make room.

285

Billy Collins once memorably described himself as a 'skeleton . . . at a typewriter' when writing a poem. 'Memento Mori' (reminder of death in Latin) is the name given to an image of death that traditionally a religious person would keep near them, often a skull. But Collins doesn't need a special object to remind him of his own mortality. He only has to look around his study to realise that all the objects in it will outlive him. I love the final image of his anglepoise lamp waddling after the coffin in Collins's funeral cortège.

When Death Comes
Mary Oliver

When death comes
like the hungry bear in autumn;
when death comes and takes all the bright coins from his purse

to buy me, and snaps the purse shut;
when death comes
like the measle-pox;

when death comes
like an iceberg between the shoulder blades,

I want to step through the door full of curiosity, wondering:
what is it going to be like, that cottage of darkness?

And therefore I look upon everything
as a brotherhood and a sisterhood,
and I look upon time as no more than an idea,
and I consider eternity as another possibility,

last orders

Mary Oliver's final thought in this poem, 'I don't want to end up simply having visited this world', has made me reread this poem many times. Use this poem as ammunition if you need to be forced out your comfort zone.

and I think of each life as a flower, as common
as a field daisy, and as singular,

and each name a comfortable music in the mouth,
tending, as all music does, toward silence,

and each body a lion of courage, and something
precious to the earth.

When it's over, I want to say: all my life
I was a bride married to amazement.
I was the bridegroom, taking the world into my arms.

When it's over, I don't want to wonder
if I have made of my life something particular, and real.
I don't want to find myself sighing and frightened,
or full of argument.

I don't want to end up simply having visited this world.

Candles

C. P. Cavafy

Days to come stand in front of us
like a row of burning candles —
golden, warm, and vivid candles.

Days past fall behind us,
a gloomy line of burnt-out candles;
the nearest are still smoking,
cold, melted, and bent.

I don't want to look at them: their shape saddens me,
and it saddens me to remember their original light.
I look ahead at my burning candles.

I don't want to turn, don't want to see, terrified,
how quickly that dark line gets longer,
how quickly one more dead candle joins another.

last orders

Cavafy died of cancer of the larynx in 1933, on the same day as he was born. His last
action was to draw a circle on a blank sheet of paper and then put a period in the middle
of the circle. This haunting poem reminds the reader to make the most of each of the days
they have allotted to them. I love the imagery of the bright candles ahead and the
smoking, extinguished ones behind.

Do not go gentle into that good night
Dylan Thomas

Do not go gentle into that good night,
Old age should burn and rave at close of day;
Rage, rage against the dying of the light.

Though wise men at the end know dark is right,
Because their words had forked no lightning they
Do not go gentle into that good night.

Good men, the last wave by, crying how bright
Their frail deeds might have danced in a green bay,
Rage, rage against the dying of the light.

Wild men who caught and sang the sun in flight,
And learned, too late, they grieved it on its way,
Do not go gentle into that good night.

Grave men, near death, who see with blinding sight
Blind eyes could blaze like meteors and be gay,
Rage, rage against the dying of the light.

And you, my father, there on the sad height,
Curse, bless me now with your fierce tears, I pray,
Do not go gentle into that good night.
Rage, rage against the dying of the light.

Here is the famous yelp of rage that Dylan Thomas once wrote in response to the news of
his father's dying.

Days
Philip Larkin

What are days for?
Days are where we live,
They come, they wake us
Time and time over.

They are to be happy in:
Where can we live but days?

Ah, solving that question
Brings the priest and the doctor
In their long coats
Running over the fields.

Another unreasonably beautiful poem about mortality from Larkin. I find the last image of the priest and the doctor in their long coats running over the fields (why fields?) puzzling and memorable in equal measure. Like all great poetry, this poem suggests far more than it explains.

Mutability
Percy Bysshe Shelley

We are as clouds that veil the midnight moon;
How restlessly they speed, and gleam, and quiver,
Streaking the darkness radiantly! – yet soon
Night closes round, and they are lost forever:

Or like forgotten lyres, whose dissonant strings
Give various response to each varying blast,
To whose frail frame no second motion brings
One mood or modulation like the last.

We rest. – A dream has power to poison sleep;
We rise. – One wandering thought pollutes the day;
We feel, conceive or reason, laugh or weep;
Embrace fond woe, or cast our cares away:

It is the same! – For, be it joy or sorrow,
The path of its departure still is free:
Man's yesterday may ne'er be like his morrow;
Nought may endure but Mutability.

Apart from the final certainty, the only other thing that can be relied on in life, as Shelley points out, is mutability. A sobering thought to anyone who likes to think they have their affairs in order.

Give Yourself a Hug
Grace Nichols

Give yourself a hug
when you feel unloved

Give yourself a hug
when people put on airs
to make you feel a bug

Give yourself a hug
when everyone seems to give you
a cold-shoulder shrug

Give yourself a hug –
a big big hug

And keep on singing
'Only one in a million like me
Only one in a million-billion-thrillion-zillion
like me.'

Grace Nichols grew up in Guyana and first came to Britain at the age of seventeen. A poet and novelist, perhaps her most successful book is The Fat Black Woman's Poems. *The collection, from which the poem is taken, lays down the gauntlet to all that is mean-spirited in Western society.*

An Epilogue
John Masefield

I have seen flowers come in stony places
And kind things done by men with ugly faces,
And the gold cup won by the worst horse at the races,
So I trust, too.

A poetic example of the power of positive thinking. Masefield was cheerfully robust about life. The epitaph he wrote for himself is similarly brisk: Let no religious rite be done or read / In any place for me when I am dead / But burn my body into ash, and scatter / The ash in secret into running water, / Or on the windy down, and let none see; / And then thank God that there's an end of me. Unfortunately these lines weren't found until after he had been installed in Poets' Corner with much pomp and ceremony.

Silence
Marianne Moore

My father used to say,
'Superior people never make long visits,
have to be shown Longfellow's grave
or the glass flowers at Harvard.
Self-reliant like the cat –
that takes its prey to privacy,
the mouse's limp tail hanging like a shoelace from its mouth –
they sometimes enjoy solitude,
and can be robbed of speech
by speech which has delighted them.
The deepest feeling always shows itself in silence;
not in silence, but restraint'.
Nor was he insincere in saying, 'Make my house your inn'.
Inns are not residences.

The full quotation that inspired this poem by the American poet Marianne Moore goes like this: 'Superior people never make long visits, then people are not so glad when you've gone.' Moore herself said that 'When I am visiting, I like to go about by myself. I never have to be shown Longfellow's grave or the glass flowers at Harvard.' I can only aspire to this level of self-reliance.

24th September 1945
Nasim Hikmet
(translated from the Turkish by Richard McKane)

The best sea: has yet to be crossed.
The best child: has yet to be born.
The best days: have yet to be lived;
and the best word that I wanted to say to you
is the word that I have not yet said.

This comes from a series of poems that the Turkish poet Nasim Hikmet wrote to his third wife Piraye during his thirteen-year imprisonment in an Istanbul jail for political dissidence. They are moving and hopeful tributes to love in adversity.

If People Disapprove of You . . .
Sophie Hannah

Make being disapproved of your hobby.
Make being disapproved of your aim.
Devise new ways of scoring points
In the Being Disapproved Of Game.

Let them disapprove in their dozens.
Let them disapprove in their hoards.
You'll find that being disapproved of
Builds character, brings rewards.

Just like any form of striving.
Don't be arrogant; don't coast
On your high disapproval rating.
Try to be disapproved of most.

At this point, if it's useful,
Draw a pie-chart or a graph.
Show it to someone who disapproves.
When they disapprove, just laugh.

Count the emotions you provoke:
Anger, suspicion, shock.
One point for each of these and two
For every boat you rock.

Feel yourself warming to your task –
You do it bloody well.
At last you've found an area
In which you can excel.

Savour the thrill of risk without
The fear of getting caught.
Whether they sulk or scream or pout,
Enjoy your new-found sport.

Meanwhile all those who disapprove
While you are having fun
Won't even know the game exists
So tell yourself you've won.

Sophie Hannah here is making fun of exhortatory poems like Kipling's 'If'. But though her intention is ironic, her advice is actually quite sound.

Sometimes
Sheenagh Pugh

Sometimes things don't go, after all,
from bad to worse. Some years, muscadel
faces down frost; green thrives; the crops don't fail;
sometimes a man aims high, and all goes well.

A people sometimes will step back from war;
elect an honest man; decide they care
enough, that they can't leave some stranger poor.
Some men become what they were born for.

Sometimes our best efforts do not go
amiss; sometimes we do as we meant to.
The sun will sometimes melt a field of sorrow
that seemed hard frozen: may it happen for you.

This poem has appeared on the London Underground, in trams in Helsinki and on the Metro in St. Petersburg. It has been read during the Irish peace negotiations and in the South African parliament, but all this acclaim has bemused the poem's author, Sheenagh Pugh, who writes: 'It wasn't political, nor is it about depression. It isn't even basically very optimistic. It was originally written about a sportsman who had a drug problem and it expressed the hope that he might eventually get over it – because things do go right sometimes . . . But it isn't anywhere near skilful or subtle enough and I would cheerfully disown it, if people didn't write to me saying that it had helped them.'

From **Macbeth**
Act V, scene v
William Shakespeare

Tomorrow, and tomorrow, and tomorrow,
Creeps in this petty pace from day to day,
To the last syllable of recorded time;
And all our yesterdays have lighted fools
The way to dusty death. Out, out, brief candle!
Life's but a walking shadow, a poor player
That struts and frets his hour upon the stage
And then is heard no more: it is a tale
Told by an idiot, full of sound and fury,
Signifying nothing.

This speech comes at the end of the play, just after Macbeth has heard of the death of his wife and before his defeat at the hands of Macduff. It is one of the few pauses in the action and sums up the fury, despair and guilt of Macbeth now he finds himself facing death.

The Slow Starter
Louis MacNeice

A watched clock never moves, they said:
Leave it alone and you'll grow up.
Nor will the sulking holiday train
Start sooner if you stamp your feet.
    He left the clock to go its way;
    The whistle blew, the train went gay.

Do not press me so, she said;
Leave me alone and I will write
But not just yet, I am sure you know
The problem. Do not count the days.
    He left the calendar alone;
    The postman knocked, no letter came.

O never force the pace, they said
Leave it alone, you have lots of time,
Your kind of work is none the worse
For slow maturing. Do not rush.
    He took their tip, he took his time,
    And found his time and talent gone.

Oh you have had your chance, It said:
Left it alone and it was one.
Who said a watched clock never moves?
Look at it now. Your chance was I.
    He turned and saw the accusing clock
    Race like a torrent round a rock.

A chilling poem about the dangers of procrastination. I keep meaning to put it up in my study . . .

You Wake Up in the Morning
Arnold Bennett

You wake up in the morning, and lo! your purse is magically filled with twenty-four hours of the magic tissue of the universe of your life. No one can take it from you. No one receives either more or less than you receive. Waste your infinitely precious commodity as much as you will, and the supply will never be withheld from you. Moreover, you cannot draw on the future. Impossible to get into debt. You can only waste the passing moment. You cannot waste tomorrow; it is kept for you.

A robust retort to the hateful phrase 'time-poor'. Everybody has the same amount of time in a day, it's what you do with it that counts.

To virgins to make much of time
Robert Herrick

Gather ye Rosebuds while ye may,
Old Time is still a-flying:
And this same flower that smiles to-day
Tomorrow will be dying.

The glorious Lamp of Heaven, the Sun,
The higher he's a-getting,
The sooner will his Race be run,
And nearer he's to Setting.

That Age is best which is the first,
When Youth and blood are warmer;
But being spent, the worse, and worst
Times, still succeed the former.

Then be not coy, but use your time,
And while ye may, go marry:
For having lost but once your prime,
You may for ever tarry.

This is a popular wedding reading with its instructions to marry rather than tarry: but what the poem is really about is making the most of the time you have left.

Ozymandias
P. B. Shelley

I met a traveller from an antique land
Who said: Two vast and trunkless legs of stone
Stand in the desert . . . Near them, on the sand,
Half sunk, a shatter'd visage lies, whose frown
And wrinkled lip and sneer of cold command,
Tell that its sculptor well those passions read
Which yet survive, stamp'd on these lifeless things,
The hand that mock'd them, and the heart that fed;
And on the pedestal these words appear:
'My name is Ozymandias, king of kings:
Look on my works, ye Mighty, and despair!'
Nothing beside remains. Round the decay
Of that colossal wreck, boundless and bare,
The lone and level sands stretch far away.

This poem was inspired by a sonnet also called 'Ozymandias' by Shelley's friend Horace Smith, which spoke of a 'gigantic Leg' in the desert, apparently a dig at George III who was famous for his sturdy pins. But anyone who saw the recent pictures of Saddam Hussein's statue being demolished by American troops will feel the contemporary resonance of this satire on the vanity of human pride and ambition.

An Arundel Tomb
Philip Larkin

Side by side, their faces blurred,
The earl and countess lie in stone,
Their proper habits vaguely shown
As jointed armour, stiffened pleat,
And that faint hint of the absurd –
The little dogs under their feet.

Such plainness of the pre-baroque
Hardly involves the eye, until
It meets his left-hand gauntlet, still
Clasped empty in the other; and
One sees, with a sharp tender shock,
His hand withdrawn, holding her hand.

They would not think to lie so long.
Such faithfulness in effigy
Was just a detail friends would see:
A sculptor's sweet commissioned grace
Thrown off in helping to prolong
The Latin names around the base.

They would not guess how early in
Their supine stationary voyage
The air would change to soundless damage,
Turn the old tenantry away;
How soon succeeding eyes begin
To look, not read. Rigidly they

Persisted, linked, through lengths and breadths
Of time. Snow fell, undated. Light
Each summer thronged the glass. A bright
Litter of birdcalls strewed the same
Bone-riddled ground. And up the paths
The endless altered people came,

Washing at their identity.
Now, helpless in the hollow of
An unarmorial age, a trough
Of smoke in slow suspended skeins
Above their scrap of history,
Only an attitude remains.

Time has transfigured them into
Untruth. The stone fidelity
They hardly meant has come to be
Their final blazon, and to prove
Our almost-instinct almost true:
What will survive of us is love.

Larkin's magnificent meditation on the way that each generation interprets the past according to its own needs and desires. The clasped hands of the figures on the tomb in Arundel church symbolises the enduring power of love to our needy, sentimental generation.

Late Fragment
Raymond Carver

And did you get what
you wanted from this life, even so?
I did.
And what did you want?
To call myself beloved, to feel myself
beloved on the earth.

*The American short-story writer and poet Raymond Carver wrote this poem for his wife,
the poet Tess Gallagher, while he was dying from a brain tumour. Carver had met Tess ten
years earlier when he was drunk, divorced and unable to write. He credited her with giving
him a second act in life. This poem is his tribute to the happiness she gave him, but I
think its meaning is universal. These are the words I want at my funeral.*

Fleur Adcock (1934–)

Maya Angelou (1928–)

Matthew Arnold (1822–1888)

Margaret Atwood (1939–)

W. H. Auden (1907–1973)

Connie Bensley (1929–)

John Betjeman (1906–1984)

Elizabeth Bishop (1911–1979)

William Blake (1757–1827)

Rupert Brooke (1887–1915)

Elizabeth Barrett Browning (1806–1861)

Robert Browning (1812–1889)

Robert Burns (1759–1796)

Lord Byron (1788–1824)

Norman Cameron (1905–1953)

Lewis Carroll (1832–1898)

Raymond Carver (1938–1988)

Charles Causley (1917–2003)

C. P. Cavafy (1863–1933)

Po Chu-I (772–846)

Kate Clanchy (1965–)

John Clare (1793–1864)

Arthur Hugh Clough (1819–1861)

Billy Collins (1941–)

Wendy Cope (1945–)

Frances Cornford (1886–1960)

E. E. Cummings (1894–1962)

W. H. Davies (1871–1940)

Dick Davis (1945–)

Emily Dickinson (1830–1886)

John Donne (1572–1631)

Ernest Dowson (1867–1900)

John Dryden (1631–1700)

Carol Ann Duffy (1955–)

Ruth Fainlight (1931–)

U. A. Fanthorpe (1929–)

Vicki Feaver (1943–)

Elaine Feinstein (1930–)

Erich Fried (1921–1988)

Robert Frost (1874–1963)

Richard le Gallienne (1866–1947)

Kahlil Gibran (1883–1931)

Robert Graves (1895–1985)

Sophie Hannah (1971–)

Thomas Hardy (1840–1928)

Tony Harrison (1937–)

Seamus Heaney (1939–)

W. E. Henley (1849–1903)

Robert Herrick (1591–1674)

Nasim Hikmet (1902–1963)

Thomas Hood (1799–1845)

A. D. Hope (1907–2000)

G. M. Hopkins (1844–1889)

A. E. Housman (1859–1936)

Jenny Joseph (1923–)

Julia Kasdorf (1962–)

John Keats (1795–1821)

Rudyard Kipling (1865–1936)

C. Lamb (1775–1834)

Philip Larkin (1922–1985)

D. H. Lawrence (1885–1930)

C. Day-Lewis (1904–1972)

Alun Lewis (1915–1944)

C. S. Lewis (1898–1963)

Michael Longley (1939–)

Robert Lowell (1917–1977)

Edward Lucie-Smith (1933–)

Myron Lysenko (1952–)

Louis MacNeice (1907–1963)

Andrew Marvell (1621–1678)

John Masefield (1878–1967)

Glyn Maxwell (1962–)

Vladimir Mayakovsky (1893–1930)

Phyllis McGinley (1905–1978)

Roger McGough (1937–)

Charlotte Mew (1869–1928)

Edna St Vincent Millay (1892–1950)

Adrian Mitchell (1932–)

Marianne Moore (1887–1972)

Edwin Morgan (1920–)

Blake Morrison (1950–)

Grace Nichols (1950–)

Pastor Niemoller (1892–1984)

John Frederick Nims (1913–1999)

Julie O'Callaghan (1954–)

Frank O'Connor (1903–1966)

Bernard O'Donoghue (1945–)

Mary Oliver (1935–)

Dorothy Parker (1893–1967)

Boris Parkin (Christopher Reid) (1949–)

Marge Piercy (1936–)

Sylvia Plath (1932–1963)

Jack Prelutsky (1940–)

Sheenagh Pugh (1950–)

Rainer Maria Rilke (1875–1926)

Alberto Rios (1952–)

Christina Rossetti (1830–1894)

Carol Rumens (1944–)

Rumi (1207–1273)

Vernon Scannell (1922–)

Anne Sexton (1928–1974)

William Shakespeare (1564–1616)

P. B. Shelley (1792–1822)

Izumi Shikibu (974–1003?)

Stevie Smith (1902–1971)

Wislawa Szymborska (1923–)

Sara Teasdale (1884–1933)

Alfred Lord Tennyson (1809–1892)

Dylan Thomas (1914–1953)

Edward Thomas (1878–1917)

R. S. Thomas (1913–2000)

Rosemary Tonks (1932–)

Derek Walcott (1930–)

Alice Walker (1944–)

Hugo Williams (1942–)

William Carlos Williams (1883–1963)

John Wilmot, Earl of Rochester (1647–1680)

William Wordsworth (1770–1850)

Thomas Wyatt (1503–1542)

W. B. Yeats (1865–1939)

Acknowledgements

Fleur Adcock: 'Things' and 'Kissing' from *Poems 1960-2000* (Bloodaxe Books, 2000), reprinted by permission of the publisher. **Maya Angelou**: 'The Telephone', 'The Health Food Diner', 'Still I Rise' and *'Ships?' from Complete Collected Poems* (Virago Press, 1994), reprinted by permission of Time Warner Books UK. **Margaret Atwood**: 'Siren Song' from *Selected Poems 1965-1975* (Virago, 1976), copyright © Margaret Atwood 1976, reprinted by permission of the publishers, Time Warner Books UK, **W H Auden**: 'Leap Before You Look', 'Roman Wall Blues', 'Lay your sleeping head my love', 'Musee des Beaux Arts', 'Gare du Midi', and 'Twelve Songs IX' ('Funeral Blues'), from W H Auden: *The Collected Poems (1976)*, reprinted by permission of the publishers, Faber & Faber Ltd. **Connie Bensley**: 'Mr and Mrs R and the Christmas Card List' from *Choosing to be a Swan* (Bloodaxe Books, 1994), reprinted by permission of the publisher. **John Betjeman**: 'Senex' from *Collected Poems (1978)*, reprinted by permission of the publishers, John Murray (Publishers) Ltd. **Elizabeth Bishop**: 'Casabianca' and 'One Art' from *The Complete Poems: 1927-1979*, copyright © 1979, 1983 by Alice Helen Methfessel, reprinted by permission of Farrar, Straus, & Giroux, LLC. **Norman Cameron**: 'The Compassionate Fool' from *Collected Poems and Selected Translations* edited by Warren Hope and Jonathan Barker (1990) reprinted by permission of the publishers, Anvil Press Poetry. **Raymond Carver**: 'Late Fragment' from *All of Us: The Collected Poems* (first published in Great Britain by Harvill, 1996), © Tess Gallagher 1996, reprinted by permission of The Random House Group Ltd. **Charles Causley**: 'Timothy Winters' from *Collected Poems* (Macmillan, 1992), reprinted by permission of David Higham Associates. **C P Cavafy**: 'Che Fece...Il Gran Rifuito', 'As Much as You Can', 'Candles', 'The City', and lines from 'Ithaka', from The Collected Poems translated by Edmund Keeley and Philip Sherrard, edited by George Savidis (The Hogarth Press, 1984), translation © Edmund Keeley and Philip Gerrard 1963, 1968, copyright © The Estate of C P Cavafy 1975, reprinted by permission of The Random House Group on behalf of the Estate of C P Cavafy. **Wang Chi**: 'Tell me now' translated by Arthur Waley from *A Hundred and Seventy Chinese Poems* (Alfred A Knopf, 1919). **Alison Chisholm**: 'Office Party' from *Daring the Slipstream* (Headland, 1997) first published in *And Somewhere a Sea...* (Southport Writers' Circle, 1991), reprinted by permission of the author. **Po Chü-i**: 'On His Baldness' translated by Arthur Waley from *Zen Poems* (Alfred A Knopf, 1999). **Kate Clanchy**: 'Two Months Gone' from Newborn (Picador, 2004), reprinted by permission of Macmillan, London, UK. **John Clare**: 'First Love' from Eric Robinson and David Powell (eds): *John Clare: The Oxford Authors* (OUP, 1984), © Eric Robinson 1984, reprinted by permission of The Curtis Brown Group Ltd, London on behalf of Eric Robinson. **Billy Collins**: 'Child Development' from *The Apple that Astonished Paris* (University of Arkansas Press, 1988), copyright © Billy Collins 1988, reprinted by permission of the publisher; 'Memento Mori' and 'Man in Space' from *Taking off Emily Dickinson's Clothes* (Picador, 2000), copyright © Billy Collins 2000, reprinted by permission of Macmillan London, UK. **Wendy Cope**: 'The New Regime', 'Bloody Men', 'Defining the Problem', and 'Flowers' from *Serious Concerns* (1992), copyright © Wendy Cope 1992, and 'The Sorrow of Socks' from As If I Don't Know (2001), copyright © Wendy Cope 2001, reprinted by permission of the publishers, Faber & Faber Ltd. **Frances Cornford**: 'To a Fat Lady Seen from the Train' from Selected Poems (Enitharmon Press, 1996), reprinted by permission of the publishers. **E E Cummings**: 'may i feel, said he' from *Complete Poems 1904-1962* edited by George J Firmage, copyright © 1991 by the Trustees for the E E Cummings Trust and George James Firmage, reprinted by permission of the publishers, W W Norton & Company. **Dick Davis**: '6 A.M. Thoughts' from *Devices and Desires: New and selected Poems 1967-1987* (1989), reprinted by permission of the publishers, Anvil Press Poetry. **W H Davies**: 'Leisure' from *Complete Poems* (Jonathan Cape, 1963), reprinted by permission of Dee & Griffin, Trustees of Mrs H M Davies Will Trust. **C. Day-Lewis**: 'Walking Away' from *The Complete Poems* (Sinclair Stevenson, 1992), copyright © 1992 in this edition The Estate of C. Day-Lewis, reprinted by permission of The Random House Group Ltd. **Emily Dickinson**: 'Wild Nights - Wild Nights!', poem 182 'Hope is the thing with feathers', poem 372 'After great pain, a formal feeling comes', and poem 919 'If I can stop one heart from breaking' from *The Poems of Emily Dickinson* edited by Ralph W Franklin (The Belknap Press of Harvard University Press, Cambridge, Mass), copyright © 1998 by the President and Fellows of Harvard College, copyright © 1951, 1955, 1979 by the President and Fellows of Harvard College, reprinted by permission of the publishers and the Trustees of Amherst College. **Carol Ann Duffy**: 'Warming her Pearls' from *Selling Manhattan* (1987), reprinted by permission of the publishers, Anvil Press Poetry; 'A Child's Sleep' copyright © Carol Ann Duffy 1995, from *Meeting Midnight* edited by Carol Ann Duffy (1999), reprinted by permission of the publishers, Faber & Faber Ltd.**U A Fanthorpe**: 'Atlas' from *Safe As Houses* (Peterloo Poets, 1995), copyright © U A Fanthorpe 1995, reprinted by permission of the publishers. Available post free

Index

Index

Visual Science
Encyclopedia

Plants

▲ Maple leaves in an Adirondack forest during autumn. The colours change as photosynthesis stops and green pigment is no longer produced. The other pigments, hidden by the chlorophyll all summer, begin to show through.

How to use this book

Every word defined in this book can be found in alphabetical order on pages 3 to 47. There is also a full index on page 48. A number of other features will help you get the most out of the *Visual Science Encyclopedia*. They are shown below.

Here you will find the first word defined on any left-hand page.

Here you will find the last word defined on any right-hand page.

Each word is shown in bold so it is easy to find.

Each new letter of the alphabet is clearly marked to help you find the word you are looking for quicker.

Other words defined in the book are highlighted in bold.

Illustrations for some words complement the text and provide further information on a topic.

Plus, many entries point to related words of interest.

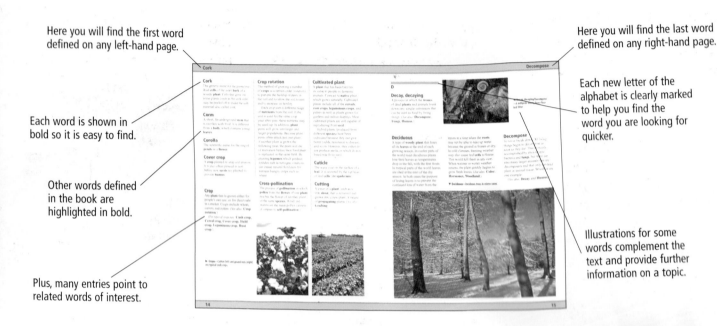

First published in 2002 by
Atlantic Europe Publishing
Company Ltd

Copyright © 2002
Atlantic Europe Publishing
Company Ltd

Author
Brian Knapp, BSc, PhD

Art Director
Duncan McCrae, BSc

Senior Designer
Adele Humphries, BA, PGCE

Editors
Lisa Magloff, BA, and
Mary Sanders, BSc

Illustrations
David Woodroffe

Designed and produced by
EARTHSCAPE EDITIONS

Reproduced in Malaysia by
Global Colour

Printed in Hong Kong by
Wing King Tong Company Ltd.

Visual Science Encyclopedia
Volume 7 *Plants*
A CIP record for this book is available from the British Library

ISBN 1-86214-039-1

Picture credits
All photographs are from the Earthscape Editions photolibrary.

This product is manufactured from sustainable managed forests. For every tree cut down, at least one more is planted.

A

Acid rain

Rain that contains a high proportion of acid gases, such as sulphur dioxide, dissolved in it. These high concentrations are not natural, but are produced as a result of burning fossil fuels, especially in power stations.

Sulphur dioxide gas is very soluble in water and cloud droplets readily absorb it. When the cloud droplets gather to make a raindrop, the raindrop is a weak acid.

Acid rain is perhaps best described as acid fallout, because the acid gases can affect **plants** when the air is dry as well as when rain falls.

Acid gases in the air are absorbed by some plants through their leaves and this also causes plants to grow poorly. In severe cases the plants will die. Some plants are especially likely to suffer. They include **coniferous trees** such as pine. Large areas of **coniferous forest** have been killed by acid rain both in northern Europe and in North America.

Acorn

The **fruit** of the oak. It consists of a hard-shelled, one-seeded **nut** held to the **stalk** by a green cap.

Adaptation, adapt

The way in which some part of a living thing makes it better able to make use of a particular

The **spines** on a **cactus** are an example of adaptation. In this case its **leaves** have become smaller, hard and pointed. As a result, the leaves lose less water and at the same time protect the **plant** from attack.

Adaptation is the result of small changes over many generations. Plants do not choose to change to match their environments. Rather, those that have features best suited to an area thrive better than others and so have more offspring.

Plants now live in many kinds of environments, but no plant can live in all environments. That is because some of the world's environments are too demanding. For example, some parts of the world have long, cold winters, while others are hot and wet throughout the year.

So, success for each **species** has been a matter of adapting to one

kind of environment. Here are just a few of the countless adaptations that plants have made.

Plants that can survive in the cold grow slowly because the temperature is too low for the chemical processes that make new tissues to work quickly. They are all **perennials** and they almost all grow close to the ground. Many have special forms of antifreeze in their leaves.

Plants that live in the warm, constant temperatures near the equator have **evergreen leaves** because there is no cold or dry season to make a plant need to shed its leaves seasonally. In a **rainforest** the constant flow of water through the soils makes them very infertile, and so rainforest plants have to adapt to find nourishment where they can. They do it by having **roots** that spread out in a fine network at the soil surface. Then, when leaves rot and release **minerals**, the growing plants can collect the nourishment before it is washed through the soil.

Plants that live in deserts have to adapt differently. They must conserve water, so they have few **pores** and small, leathery leaves. Many have **stems** that hold water and spines to protect the stems from attack by animals searching for the water they store.

Plants living in cooler areas have adapted by shedding their leaves in the autumn and then laying **dormant** through the winter. (*See also:* **Deciduous**.)

◀ **Acorn** – Acorns fall in large numbers beside an oak tree, and seedlings have to compete with one another for survival.

Adventitious roots

Roots that grow out from the **stems** of some **plants**. They are used to help support the plant and keep it from being knocked over. They are sometimes called prop roots. Adventitious roots form all along the stems of ivy plants and help stabilise them as the plants climb. (See **tendril** for a different way in which some plants attach themselves to supports.) (*See also:* **Climbing plants**.)

Alpine plants need to store as much heat as possible. Many are tufted, have furry leaves, and grow in dense, low bushes. Many even make their own antifreeze. The leaves are dark green to soak up as much of the Sun's heat as possible.

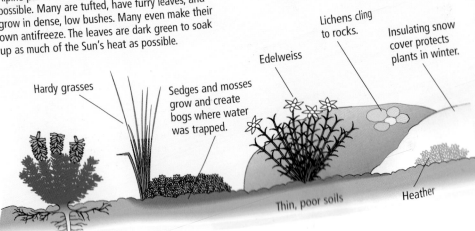

▼ **Alpine** – Adaptations of some alpine plants.

Hardy grasses

Sedges and mosses grow and create bogs where water was trapped.

Edelweiss

Lichens cling to rocks.

Insulating snow cover protects plants in winter.

Thin, poor soils

Heather

◄ **Aerial root** – These aerial roots, also known as prop roots, belong to mangroves.

Aerating root

A **root** that rises above water to allow a **plant** to absorb air. Mangroves are an example of a plant with aerating roots.

Aerial roots

Roots that form from **stems** high above the ground. They may be used to attach a **plant** to a surface, as in the case of a **vine**, or they may be rooting **shoots**, which will help feed the plant when they reach the ground. (*See also:* **Aerating root** and **Epiphyte**.)

Air plant

(*See:* **Epiphyte**.)

Algae

Microscopically small, simple, plant-like living things found in water or in damp places such as tree **trunks**. Algae are so small that they have no roots, stems, or **leaves**.

Algae are blue-green, red, or brown and contain a substance called **chlorophyll** that allows them to make energy using sunlight. Algae occur in vast numbers and provide food for many sea and freshwater animals. (Scientists put algae in a separate biological **kingdom** called protista.)

(*See also:* **Epiphyte** and **Evolution, plant**.)

Algal bloom

The growth of such huge numbers of **algae** that they cause the colour of the water to change.

Algae exist in most waters, but because they are so small, they are invisible except with the aid of a microscope. However, algae begin to reproduce very rapidly if there is enough nourishment in the water. That can happen, for example, when a storm at sea stirs up the seabed and mixes **minerals** with the sea water. It can also happen when nourishment is artificially added to the water, such as when fertilisers drain into lakes and rivers from nearby fields, or when raw sewage is allowed to flow into water.

When algae bloom in a closed lake or slow-flowing water, they take oxygen from the water. This may make it impossible for other **plants** and for most animals to live. Without animals to break down dead plant and animal tissue, **decaying** material only partly decomposes and also gives off powerful fumes

Alpine

The name given to **plants** that can survive the harsh conditions of high mountains where there are prolonged snowfall, frequent frost, stony soils, high winds and intense sun. They are named after the Alps mountains of Europe. Alpine plants are low and slow growing, and often flower quickly as soon as the snows melt. They are all **perennials**. Many alpine plants are similar to those plants that grow in the arctic, known as tundra plants.

▶ **Alpine** – All alpine plants need to be adapted for dry conditions. That may seem strange, when they may be covered in snow for half the year. But the water in snow is locked up as ice, and so plants cannot use it. Then, as soon as the snow melts, harsh winds dry out the ground. To cope with this, even plants that seem tiny when seen on the surface may have deep taproots that search for water far underground.

Anaerobic

Without oxygen. It is possible for some **plants** to grow in water that is stagnant and contains very little oxygen. However, the energy released in this kind of environment is small and so plants grow slowly. That is why there is so little growth in a stagnant pond.

Anchor root

A large **root** that holds a **plant** in place in the soil. **Taproots** are one type of anchor root.

Angiosperm

An older scientific name for **flowering plants**, now replaced by the word anthophyta. This group of **plants** has **flowers** that are usually **pollinated** by insects, bats and humming-birds, and **seeds** that are formed inside a **fruit**. There are about 230,000 **species** of angiosperm worldwide. (*See also:* **Seed plants**.)

Annual

A **flowering plant** that completes its **life cycle** (**germination**, growth, flowering, setting **seed** and finally dying) in a single growing season (but not necessarily a year). This allows the plant to make use of the warm or wet time of the year, so that it does not have to be **adapted** to cope with long periods of cold or dry weather (as is the case with the other major group of plants, the **perennials**).

The word annual was first used to describe plants in temperate climates, where the growing season occurs just once a year, hence the term annual. However, in some other environments, such as in hot deserts, the growing season occurs whenever it rains, which can be more than once a year or only once every several years.

Annuals do not grow in places without seasons (for example, tropical **rainforests**). (*See also:* **Colonise** and **Herbaceous plants**.)

▶ **Annual** – The stages of the poppy, a well-known annual plant. From left to right: bud; open flower with pollen; pollinated flower dying back; seed pod developed at base of flower.

Anther

The swollen end of the male **stamen** inside a **flower**. The anther is normally in the shape of a pad that produces **pollen** grains. The pollen grains are brushed off the surface of the anther each time an animal searches for **nectar** inside a flower. (*See also:* **Filament** and **Pollination**.)

Aquatic plant

A **plant** growing in water.

Arboreal

A word that means tree-like or tree-dwelling.

Association

A name given to a **community** of **plants** that occur together. The association is normally named after the largest member, often a **tree**. For example, in a **woodland** the most common tree might be an oak. In this case the association would be called an oak woodland. The other plants that might grow with the oak include holly, brambles, grass, primroses and so on.

B

Bark

The outer layers of a **woody stem**. The inner bark is soft and contains the growing layer and the tubes that carry food and water from the **roots** to the **leaves** (*see:* **Xylem**). The outer bark is harder and made mainly of dead **cork tissue**. The **cells** of this tissue contain fatty substances that stop air and water from passing through them. They also protect the inner growing bark from damage by storm, fire and animals. Plants that have to survive frequent fires often have very thick bark. The giant redwood **trees** have massive barks for this reason.

The outermost layers of the bark often split as the stem grows. In time they may flake off.

Many tree **species** can be identified from the character of their bark alone. **Herbaceous** stems do not have bark. (*See also:* **Cork**; **Resin**; **Rubber**.)

▲ **Berry** – Scientifically, the banana is a berry.

Berry (part of a plant)

A simple, fleshy **fruit** containing many **seeds**. Scientifically, the cranberry, the banana, the orange, the lime, the cucumber, the water-melon, the date and the tomato are all berries.

Raspberries, blackberries and strawberries are not true berries (simple fruits) but collections of fruits. Scientifically they are called **drupes**.

Berry (food)

Any small, edible fleshy **fruit**, such as cherry, blackberry, raspberry and strawberry.

Biennial

A **flowering plant** that has a **life cycle** that takes two years to complete. Wallflowers, celery and cabbage are examples of biennials, but celery and cabbage flowers are usually not seen because the plants are harvested during their first year. (*See also:* **Herbaceous plants**.)

Blade

The thin, usually flat part that makes up the bulk of a **leaf**. The rest of the leaf is made up of the **stalk**. The blade is strengthened by a pattern of **veins**.

Blades have many shapes, depending on the needs of the **plant**. For example, blades of the giant water lily have upturned edges so that the blade floats on the water like a boat. (*See also:* **Evergreen**.)

Botany

The science of plants.

Bract

Leaf-like structures that surround small **flowers** (**florets**) and give the impression of **petals**. They help attract insects and other pollinators. Some bracts are green, but others are brightly coloured as, for example, tropical bougainvillea **plants** or the poinsettias used as **houseplants** at Christmas. (*See also:* **Composite flower**.)

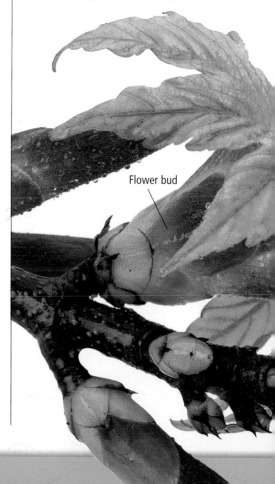

Flower bud

Branch(es)

A woody **stem** that grows off the **trunk**, or main stem, of a woody **plant**. The branching pattern is often one of the most noticeable features of a **shrub** or **tree**. For example, the branches of a poplar stay close to the trunk, giving it a very narrow appearance, while the branches of an oak spread out and make the tree about as wide as it is tall. (*See also:* **Twig**.)

Broad-leaved trees

Trees that have flat **leaf blades**. Some broad-leaved trees are **deciduous** and shed their leaves seasonally, while others are **evergreen**. Most broad-leaved trees would also be called **hardwoods**.

Bud

A part of a **plant shoot** that contains a short piece of **stem** surrounded by young **leaves**. Some buds simply grow long shoots that make a plant taller or broader, while others develop **flowers** (*see:* **Flower bud**). In this case the bud contains young **petals** rather than young leaves.

(*See also:* **Hormones; Lateral bud; Life cycle; Reproductive growth; Sepal; Terminal bud.**)

Bulb

The resting stage of some **flowering plants**. It consists of a short **stem** surrounded by **leaves**. When the plant stops resting and bursts into growth, these leaves will push out of the top of the bulb, while the central **shoot** will grow into a **stalk**. The leaves of a bulb act as food storage, enabling the plant to begin to grow at the start of a growing season, before the **roots** can supply nourishment. Lilies, hyacinths and onions are examples of plants that grow from bulbs.

◀ **Bulb** – A hyacinth bulb.

◀ **Bud** – Buds and flowers of a horsechestnut.

Leaf bud

▼ **Bulb** – A daffodil, showing the way the bulb produces clones.

Short stem surrounded by leaves

Roots

Clone

Burr

A name for any kind of **seed** case that has hooks on it, and that will attach to the fur of passing animals. Burrs are a common and very effective means of carrying seeds to new environments.

Bush

A low **shrub**, especially of the kind that has many **branches** and **leaves** and is relatively compact in shape. The term is also used for a region of wilderness where the main kinds of **plants** are shrubs.

Buttress root

A special shape of **tree root** that comes off the **trunk** above ground. Buttress roots are often thin and plank-like. Buttress roots help support tall trees; by sending roots out farther from the trunk, they also help the tree reach nourishment from a wider area. Almost all buttress roots grow on tropical trees.

▼ **Cactus** – How the saguaro cactus is adapted to survive.

The cactus stores water in its stem.

There are no leaves to reduce the amount of water lost to the hot, dry desert air.

▶ **Buttress root** – Some tropical rainforest trees have buttress roots.

To protect it against animals, this cactus has spines, but they can only be seen close up.

C

Cactus, cacti

A woody-stemmed **perennial flowering plant** (also called a **succulent**) that usually has **spines** (rather than **leaves**) and produces brightly coloured **flowers**. They grow in dry desert conditions. To minimise water loss, leaves small or missing.

◀ **Canopy** – The tropical rainforest canopy is so complete that little light filters through, and the trees have no lower branches or leaves.

takes over the role of making food and energy from sunlight that leaves would otherwise perform.

Many **cells** in the cactus are specially developed to store water.

Cactus **roots** are usually **fibrous** and shallow, forming a net of roots that allows them to gather any rain seeping into the ground over a wide area. (*See also:* **Adaptation** and **Houseplant**.)

Calyx
The scientific name for the cup-shaped base of a **flower** formed by small **sepals**.

Cambium
The thin layer of growing **cells** just below the hard part of the **bark** in a **woody plant**. The cells add to the width of the **stem**, producing a pair of layers each growing season. These layers form rings of growth that can be seen when a plant is cut down. (*See also:* **Life cycle** and **Seasonal rings**.)

Canopy
The covering of **leaves** that forms when tall **trees** grow close together. The height of the canopy varies widely. The canopy is highest in the equatorial **rainforest**, where trees are commonly 40m or more tall. The canopy leaves cut off most of the direct sunlight from the ground, making it difficult for **plants** to grow below.

Carbohydrate
A main form of **plant tissue**. It contains carbon, hydrogen and oxygen. **Sugar** is a soluble form of carbohydrate and **starch** is a less soluble form. (*See also:* **Cellulose** and **Grain**.)

Carnivorous plant
A **plant** that has become **adapted** to capture small animals, particularly insects, by using modified leaves that act as traps and pitchers. Once the animal is trapped, it is then digested by chemicals (enzymes) released by the plant.

The purpose of trapping animals is to help the plant survive in places where the soil is very poor, and where otherwise it would be difficult to get enough

▼▶ **Carnivorous plant** – A pitcher plant has a smooth and slippy inner surface. As soon as an insect lands on the rim and ventures slightly inwards, the insect falls into the liquid of the pitcher.

nourishment from the soil. Such **nutrient**-poor places include peat bogs and heaths. Nitrogen is one of the most important nutrients that carnivorous plants get from animals.

Pitcher plants capture prey by using a liquid-filled pitfall. The animal is attracted to the pitfall because of the scent of the liquid. Once on the lip, the animal reaches a smooth part of the pitfall, loses its grip and falls in. The smooth, vertical sides then prevent it from escaping. Sundews and flytraps (for example, Venus flytrap) have active trapping systems. When the animal lands on the surface, it is often trapped by a glue produced on the surface of the leaves. As the animal struggles, tiny hairs on the trap send a chemical signal and the leaves close. (*See also:* **Turgor movements**.)

Most carnivorous plants are small, **herbaceous perennials**.

◀ **Carnivorous plant** – This cross-section shows insects trapped in the liquid inside a pitcher plant.

9

Carpel

A modified, **seed**-carrying, rolled-up leaf. One or more carpels make up the **pistil**. The pistil of a sweet pea is made of just one carpel, but a mustard flower has a pistil made of two carpels. Lilies have pistils made of three carpels.

Cash crop

A **crop** that is produced for direct sale to markets. Cotton and tobacco are cash crops.

Cell

The tiny building blocks of all life. All but the simplest kinds of **plants** contain many kinds of cells, each specialised for a particular role. (*See also:* **Cellulose**; **Epidermis**; **Guard cells**; **Nucleus**; **Tissue**.)

Cellulose

An insoluble form of **carbohydrate** that forms the walls of **plant cells** and gives them strength and a degree of stiffness.

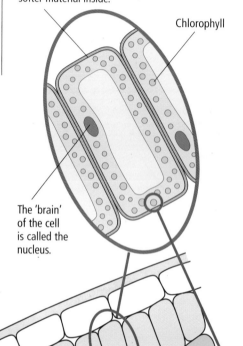

The wall of each cell is made from a tough material called cellulose that protects the softer material inside.

Chlorophyll

The 'brain' of the cell is called the nucleus.

Flat, almost square cells make up the outer tissue of a leaf (epidermis). The cells fit together tightly to protect the other cells inside the leaf. They also secrete a waxy coat onto the surface, making the leaf waterproof (cuticle).

Surface of leaf

Chlorophyll

Guard cells open to let air and water vapour move in and out of the leaf pore.

Vein cells

Underside of leaf

▲ **Cell** – A cross-section of part of a leaf showing the main function of the cells.

Cereal

Any member of the grass family of **plants** that produces starchy **seeds** that can be used for food. Cereals are also called **grains**.

The cereals most commonly grown are barley, maize, millet, oats, rice, rye, sorghum and wheat.

Wheat is the cereal grown most widely across the world. It is used as flour for bread, pasta, cakes and so on, as well as in whole grain form for breakfast cereals and breads. It grows best in temperate climates.

Rice is the second most widely grown cereal and is the primary grain **crop** in Asia. Rice can be grown in flooded fields (paddy rice) or on dry soil (dry rice). Rice has to be milled before it can be used. Some rice is used for breakfast cereal.

Rye is widely used for bread-making. It is grown on poor soils and can grow in areas with severe winters. Eastern Europe is the main rye-growing area of the world.

Oats are another temperate crop.

Chlorophyll

A green substance (**pigment**) found in leaf and some stem **cells** that can trap some of the energy in sunlight and use it to cause chemical changes that convert carbon dioxide to food (**carbohydrate**). (*See also:* **Colour**; **Leaf, leaves**; **Photosynthesis**.)

Citrus

The name for a group (**genus**) of **plants** that have pulpy **fruits** covered with thick skins. Lemons, limes, oranges, tangerines and grapefruit are all in this group. The juice has a particularly sharp, acid taste.

They are mostly grown as an animal feed and also as a breakfast cereal.

▼ **Cereal** – Ears of wheat.

▲ **Cereal** – Rice being grown on terraces in Bali.

Barley is another crop of temperate climates and will grow in cooler, wetter conditions than wheat. It is used for animal feed and for beer, whisky and breakfast foods.

Maize is originally a crop of South America. It needs warmer and drier summers than wheat. It is used for animal food, for human consumption and to make chemicals.

Sorghum and millet will grow in hot regions with an unreliable, low rainfall. They are important crops in places such as the Sahel of Africa, where people cannot grow corn reliably.

Cereal crop

Any **crop** belonging to the grass family that is grown for its **seeds** (**grains**). **Cereal** crops include rice, wheat, maize and barley.

Classification

A way of grouping living things into those with similar characteristics. By doing this, it is easier to see the relationships among them. The largest division of a classification of living things is the **kingdom**. Divisions of kingdoms include phyla, classes, orders, families, **genera** and **species**.

Climbing plants

Plants that have **stems** too weak to be self-supporting, so they attach themselves to other objects like walls or tree stems in order to grow and reach more light. Ivy (hedera) is a common climbing plant.

(*See also:* **Adventitious roots**; **Tendril**; **Vine**.)

Clone

A **plant** produced by a **cell** from its parent that has features identical to its parent. (*See also:* **Reproduction**; **Self-pollination**.)

Colonise

To grow in a new area; to move to a new place. **Plants** colonise new areas in several ways. They may produce **seeds** or **spores** that can be carried in the wind or by animals. They may also send out **runners** above or below the ground. Small plantlets grow from the runners at a distance from the parent plant.

Colonisation is fastest with transport by the wind. Many **annual** plants will colonise a bare area very quickly. (*See also:* **Weed**.)

Colour

The colour of a **plant** depends on the chemicals inside it.

A coloured chemical is called a **pigment**. The most common pigment in a plant is **chlorophyll**, which produces a green colour. Chlorophyll is present in the **stem** and **leaves**, but not in the **roots** and rarely in the **flowers**. Flowers contain other pigments. Carotene, for example, is responsible for the bright yellow colour of some **petals**.

In **deciduous** plants the leaves change colour just before they fall off because the chlorophyll begins to decompose. This allows the other coloured pigments to show through.

Community

A group of **plants** that live together with animals in an area of similar climate. Communities occur in all sizes. **Rainforest** is a very large-scale community, while smaller-scale communities may simply be the plants that grow in a valley. (*See also:* **Association** and **Habitat**.)

Composite flower

A **plant** that has a mass of small **flowers** or **florets**, but which appears to be a distinct flower. The flower head is surrounded by small, modified leaves called **bracts**. The flowers in the outermost row of the head are flat-bladed and give the impression of petals. The 'petals' of a daisy or sunflower are not **petals** at all, but the outermost modified florets.

Cone

The equivalent of a **flower** for **conifers**. It is a cone-shaped mass of papery scales. **Coniferous trees** have male cones, which carry **pollen** and female cones, which develop **seeds** (*see:* **Pollination**). Some trees have very small cones, while others, such as the sugar pine, have giant cones that can be 20cm or more long.

◀ **Cone** – A cone opened to allow seeds to escape.

A cone is a modified shoot with a spiral of pollen- or seed-bearing scales. In conifers the male and female parts are produced on separate cones. Male and female cones are borne on the same tree. The male cone is usually smaller than the female cone.

Seeds or cones are a highly concentrated source of nourishment and are an important food source for many animals, such as birds and squirrels. Squirrel-gnawed cones are often found scattered at the base of trees. All of these cones are female cones because they carry the seeds.

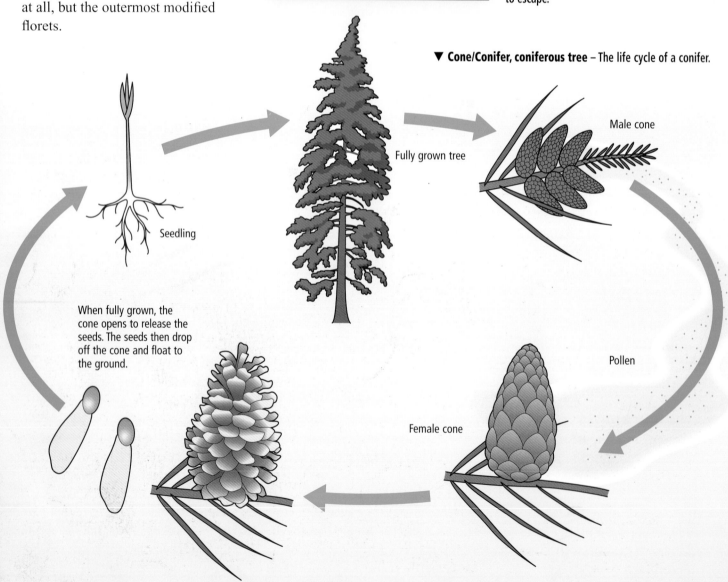

▼ **Cone/Conifer, coniferous tree** – The life cycle of a conifer.

Seedling

Fully grown tree

Male cone

Pollen

Female cone

When fully grown, the cone opens to release the seeds. The seeds then drop off the cone and float to the ground.

Conifer, coniferous tree

Any **plant** that bears its **seeds** and **pollen** on separate **cones**. Conifers belong to the plant group called **gymnosperms**, meaning that their seeds grow without the protection of a **fruit** (as is the case for **flowering plants**). Most conifers are **evergreen trees** with needle-shaped leaves.

Conifers grow everywhere in the world except for Antarctica, but are most common away from the tropics. They include firs, cedars, cypresses, junipers, larches, pines, spruces, yews, redwoods and hemlocks.

Conifer **trunks** do not contain tiny water- and **mineral**-bearing tubes of the kind found in flowering plants. Instead, they have simple **cells** connected by passages. This is what gives the **wood** its sponge-like

◄ **Conifer, coniferous tree** – This is the world's oldest tree, the bristle-cone pine.

appearance. (*See also:* **Softwood**.) The **leaves** are **needles** and usually contain canals filled with resin. The scent from the resin in the leaves and the trunk can be powerful on a warm summer's day. Most conifers are evergreen, but some, such as larch and bald cypress, are **deciduous**.

Conifers have many water-conserving **adaptations** that allow them to survive in places with a

dry climate (such as the Mediterranean and American Southwest) and also in places that have long winters when the ground is frozen hard (such as the northern **coniferous forests** and high mountains). The leaves have a thick, waxy surface layer with **pores** below the leaf surface. (*See also:* **Evolution, plant**.)

Coniferous forest

A type of vegetation dominated by **conifers**. It is mainly found in cool climatic regions and in higher mountainous regions.

(*See also:* **Acid rain**.)

▼ **Conifer, coniferous tree** – Conifers are well adapted for long, cold winters and deep snowfalls.

► **Coniferous forest** – Most coniferous forests are managed, with trees spaced more closely than would be the case if the trees grew naturally.

Cork

The general name for the protective dead **cells** of the outer **bark** of a woody **plant**. Cells that grow on some plants (such as the cork oak) may be peeled off to make the soft material also called cork.

Corm

A short, fat underground **stem** that is swollen with food. It is different from a **bulb**, which contains young **leaves**.

Corolla

The scientific name for the ring of **petals** in a **flower**.

Cover crop

A **crop** planted to stop soil erosion. It is also often ploughed in just before new **seeds** are planted to provide **humus**.

Crop

Any **plant** that is grown either for people's own use or for direct sale in a market. Crops include wheat, carrots and cotton.

(*See also:* **Crop rotation**.)

(*For types of crops see:* **Cash crop**; **Cereal crop**; **Cover crop**; **Field crop**; **Leguminous crop**; **Root crop**.)

Crop rotation

The method of growing a number of **crops** in a certain order (rotation) to prevent the buildup of pests in the soil and to allow the soil to rest and to increase its fertility.

Each crop uses a different range of **nutrients** from the soil. If the soil is used for the same crop year after year, these nutrients may be used up. In addition, **plant** pests will grow into larger and larger populations. Because plant pests often attack just one plant, if another plant is grown the following year, the pests will die of starvation before their food plant is replanted in the same field. By planting **legumes**, which produce nodules rich in nitrogen, rotations can create natural fertilisers for nutrient-hungry crops such as wheat.

Cross-pollination

The process of **pollination** in which **pollen** from the **flower** of one **plant** reaches the flower of another plant of the same **species**. Wind and insects are the main pollen carriers.
(*Compare with:* **Self-pollination**.)

Cultivated plant

A **plant** that has been bred for its value to people or domestic animals. Contrast with a **native** plant, which grows naturally. Cultivated plants include all of the **cereals**, **root crops**, **leguminous crops** and beans as well as plants grown for gardens and indoor displays. Most cultivated plants are still capable of reproducing from **seed**.

Hybrid plants (produced from different **species**) have been cultivated because they can give better yields, resistance to disease and so on. However, they either do not produce seeds or do not breed true from seed.

Cuticle

The waxy coat on the surface of a **leaf**. It is secreted by the top layer of leaf **cells** (the **epidermis**).

Cutting

A piece of a **plant**, such as a side **shoot**, that is removed and grown into a new plant. A means of **propagating** plants.
(*See also:* **Grafting**.)

▶ **Crops** – Cotton (left) and groundnuts (right) are typical cash crops.

Pollen grain

The contents of a pollen grain move down the female part of the flower.

▶ **Fertilisation** – After pollination fertilisation occurs, and seeds begin to swell at the bottom of the flower. The petals wither.

Fertilisation takes place, and the seed develops in the female part of the flower.

Seed grows

The fruit begins to form.

Petal withers

The fruit is formed.

Fibre
A solid thread that grows inside a **shoot** or **root** and gives the **plant** support.

Fibrous root
A thin **root** that may branch from a **taproot** or may be part of a mass of roots that branch from the base of the **stem**.

Field crop
Any farm **crop** (such as hay and wheat) that is grown over large areas, and that can be tended by large machines. It contrasts with a market garden crop, which is grown in small areas.

Filament
The long, thin part of the male **stalk** or **stamen** inside a **flower** that supports the **pollen**-producing **anther**.

Floret
A small **flower**, usually one of many that form a dense cluster and make up the head of a **composite flower**. (*See also:* **Bract**.)

▲ **Floret** – Individual florets after fertilisation are clearly seen in this sunflower head.

Flower

The structure that contains the **seed-producing** parts of a **flowering plant**. The most obvious parts of a flower are the thin sheets of **tissue** called **petals**. The ring of petals is called the **corolla**.

Inside the petals are the male and female parts of a flower that will produce seeds. They are the central female **pistil** and the surrounding male **stamens**. The petals are supported by short green leaves called **sepals** (*see also:* **Calyx**).

Some flowers are not single flowers, but are made of many small flowers called **florets**. The daisy family is like this. Other flowers are surrounded by modified leaves, often brightly coloured, called **bracts**.

Flowers that do not have either sepals or petals are known as incomplete.

Some plants have separate male and female flowers.

(*See also:* **Colour; Fertilisation; Flower bud; Hormones; Life cycle; Nectary; Pollen; Pollination; Reproductive growth; Turgor movements.**)

▶ **Flower** – The female parts of the flower are shown with pink lines and the male parts with blue. (See individual entries for more on each part.)

▶ **Flower** – The lily has a well-defined stigma and stamen with strong orange-coloured pollen covering the anthers.

Stigma

Style

Pistil

Ovary

Sepal (the sepals form the cup-shaped calyx)

Stalk

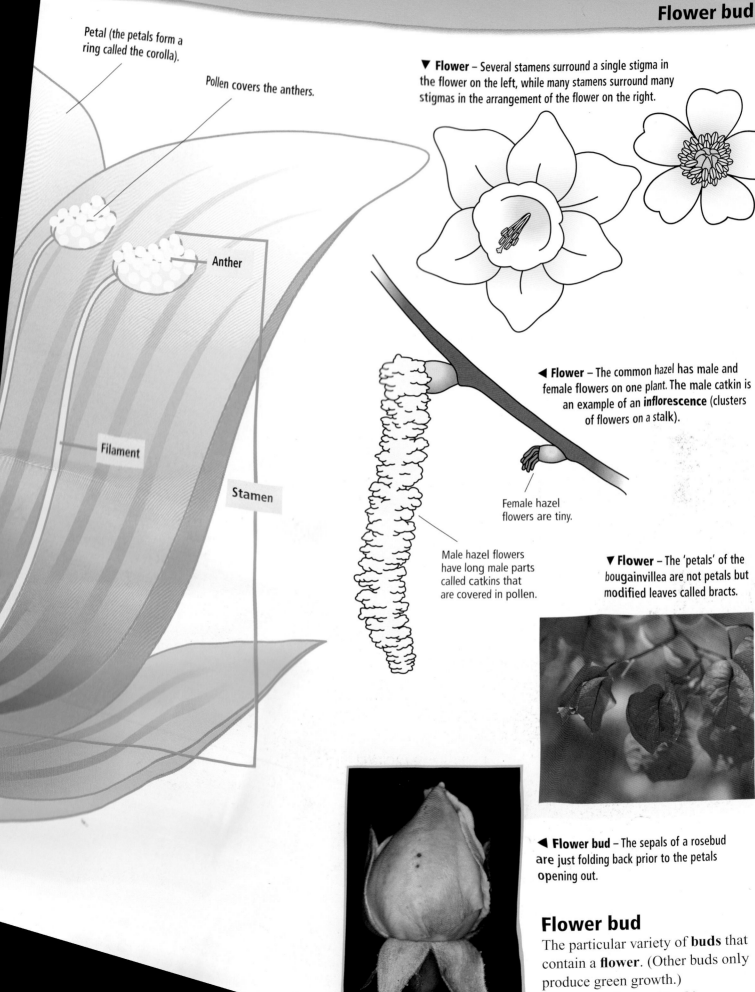

Petal (the petals form a ring called the corolla).

Pollen covers the anthers.

Anther

Filament

Stamen

▼ **Flower** – Several stamens surround a single stigma in the flower on the left, while many stamens surround many stigmas in the arrangement of the flower on the right.

◀ **Flower** – The common *hazel* has male and female flowers on one plant. The male catkin is an example of an **inflorescence** (clusters of flowers on a stalk).

Female hazel flowers are tiny.

Male hazel flowers have long male parts called catkins that are covered in pollen.

▼ **Flower** – The 'petals' of the *bougainvillea* are not petals but modified leaves called bracts.

◀ **Flower bud** – The sepals of a rosebud are just folding back prior to the petals opening out.

Flower bud

The particular variety of **buds** that contain a **flower**. (Other buds only produce green growth.)

(*See also:* **Lateral bud.**)

Flowering plant

A **plant** that produces **flowers** and **fruits** containing **seeds**. Flowering plants are called 'anthophyta (**angiosperms**) by scientists. They developed from **gymnosperms** (a group that includes **conifers**) about 130 million years ago (*see:* **Evolution, plant**).

Flowers are specialised shoots that contain thin leaves called **petals** and a seed-bearing centre (called an **ovary**).

The seeds of flowering plants are protected much more from the environment than the seeds of conifers, and this gives them a competitive advantage, which is how they came to dominate many environments. Flowering plants also tend to make more use of insects, birds and bats to carry **pollen** from one seed to another. This is a more efficient way of reproducing than allowing the pollen simply to drift in the wind.

Flowering plants have more complicated food and water systems than conifers. Food and water are carried between **leaf**, **stem** and root by means of tiny tubes (*see:* **Vascular system**). Flowering plants also contain an especially **nutrient** rich kind of **tissue** that is packed into seeds. This gives them a better chance of growth than a conifer seed.

The extremely rich nutrients in the seed tissue of flowering plants are what makes them of such value to people and are why we harvest the seeds (**grain**) from **cereal** grasses more commonly than the **cones** from **coniferous trees**.

There are two kinds of flowering plants: those that have one leaf when they **germinate** (called the **monocotyledons**), and those that have two leaves (called the **dicotyledons**). 'One-leaf' plants also differ from 'two-leaf' plants in the kind of **veins** in their leaves and in how many parts there are in the flowers. 'One-leaf' plants have flower parts in multiples of three, and 'two-leaf' plants have flower parts in multiples of four or five.

Flowering plants are made of a **shoot** (stem and leaves) and a **root**. Plants such as **trees** and **shrubs** are called woody plants. They live for many years and keep their shoot alive from one season to another without dying back. **Herbaceous plants** are those with soft, flexible shoots that die back each year.

Some flowering plants are **deciduous** and drop their leaves after each growing season, while others are **evergreen** and keep their leaves until new leaves form.

Annuals are herbaceous plants that complete their entire **life cycle** in one growing season. **Biennials** are herbaceous plants that complete their life cycle in two seasons, blooming during the second season.

Most herbaceous plants are annuals, but a few are **perennials**.

Foliage plants

Plants that are kept in the house largely for their decorative **leaves**. Favourites include the rubber plant (ficus elastica) and the Swiss cheese plant (monstera, a **climbing plant**). They are glossy, large-leaved plants that will tolerate the dry air of modern central heating. Coleus (sometimes called painted nettle) is a plant with strikingly coloured leaves.

Various palms are also good foliage plants. Begonias, while having **flowers**, are grown mainly for their mottled leaves. The spider plant (chlorophytum) has striped leaves and is even good at collecting the dust from modern offices.

Forest

A large area of **trees** with no artificial boundaries.

Form

The shape of a **plant**.

The great range of plant shapes comes from the different ways in which they grow. Some plants hug the ground; some are tall, **woody perennial** plants; some die back to a crown of **buds** over winter or during drought; some die back completely underground; some grow in water but remain attached to the bottom; some are free floating; and some are **annuals** that grow for only one season.

◄ **Foliage plant** – This **one** is variegated.

Fruit (part of a plant)

The swollen and fleshy structure that develops at the base of a **flower**. It contains the **seeds**. In some cases the fruit is thick and fleshy. An apple is one example of a fleshy fruit. In other cases the fruit is hard and dry. A poppy case is an example of a dry fruit. (*See also:* **Citrus**; **Fertilisati**

Fruit (food)

Any fleshy fruit that is eaten on its own. Apples, pears, oranges, cherries, blackberries and strawberries are all fruits. Fruits are important sources of fibre and vitamin C. (*See also:* **Berry**.)

Fungi

A plant-like living thing that produces **spores** and feeds on the **decaying** bodies of **plants** and animals. Mushrooms are one

Grafting

The process in which a **cutting** from a **woody shoot**, called a scion, is grown in the stump of a second woody **plant**, called a stock.

type of fungi. Scientists classify all fungi in their own biological **kingdom** – fungi.

▼ **Fungi** – Fungi emerging from a forest floor.

Grain

The edible **seed** of **cereal plants**. Most grains are rich in **carbohydrates** and energy and low in protein. They do not contain calcium or vitamin A, both of which are essential to human health. For this reason, flour (ground grain) is often enriched with these substances.

Guard cells

The special **cells** at the entrance to a **leaf pore**, or **stoma**, that change shape to open or close the pore.

Gymnosperms

A group of **plants** that includes the **conifers**. The word means 'naked seeds'. The **seeds** are exposed on the surface of **cone** scales, not protected inside a **fruit** (as in **angiosperms**). Gymnosperms are an older group of plant than angiosperms (from which the **flowering plants** evolved) and include the redwoods (sequoia), the largest living thing on Earth. (*See also:* **Evolution, plant** and **Seed plants**.)

G

Genus

A group of more or less similar but not identical **plants** that usually includes more than one **species**.

Germinate, germination

The process in which a **seed** takes in water and breaks open its outer casing to release the **root** and **shoot** and becomes a **seedling**. (*See also:* **Hormones** and **Life cycle**.)

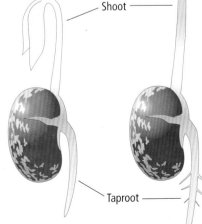

Shoot

Taproot

◀ **Germinate, germination** – This sequence shows a runner bean germinating, producing first a root, then a shoot that quickly opens to reveal a pair of leaves.

H

Habitat
The environment around a **plant**. A habitat is a small area of other plants and animals that all live together in a **community** and share the same weather and soil conditions.

▶▼ **Habitat** – Most alpine plants (right) find warmth and shelter in-between the rocks of the mountains and tundra. The organ-pipe cactus (below) has a habitat that needs freely draining soils in areas not exposed to frost.

Hardwood
The name given to **wood** primarily from **broad-leaved trees** such as oak, ash and eucalyptus. Some hardwood is actually soft (as in the case of balsa), but most hardwoods have very compact **cells**, the result of growing slowly.

Herb (plant)
Any **flowering plant** that does not have woody **stems** and that dies back at the end of the growing season. Herbs can be **annuals, biennials,** or **perennials. Herbaceous plants** often have colourful **leaves** and may be grown together to make an herbaceous border in a garden.

Herb (cooking and medicine)
A **plant** or a part of a plant that gives a special taste to food, has an attractive smell (because of the **oils** that evaporate from its **leaves**), or is thought to have special qualities in curing people of illness.

Herbaceous plants
Flowering plants with soft, flexible **shoots** that die back each year. **Annuals, biennials** and some **perennials** are herbaceous. (*See also:* **Herb (plant)**.)

Hormones

Chemical messengers that control the speed of processes throughout the whole plant (just as hormones control many processes in a human body). **Plants** contain a wide range of hormones.

Abscisic acid is a hormone that works when a plant is put under stress, such as during a drought. It causes the **pores** to close and generally begins to shut the plant down so that it conserves its moisture.

Auxins are hormones that help control the growth of plants at their **root** tips and **stem** tips. They are also active in controlling **fruit** production and the shedding of **leaves** (in **deciduous** plants).

Cytokinins are the hormones that cause a **seed** to **germinate**, making the single seed **cell** divide and divide again until it has formed a whole plant. They also help **buds** form and **shoots** grow each season.

Gibberellins are hormones that trigger **flower** development.

(*See also:* **Life cycle**.)

Houseplant

A **plant** that can be grown successfully indoors. The best houseplants are those that are attractive to look at and easy to care for. They include the bromeliads, **cacti**, **ferns**, begonias and palms. African violets, poinsettias and similar plants tend to be seasonal favourites.

Humus

The decomposed or **decayed** remains of **plants**. It is a black, slippery substance that contains a wealth of **nutrients** in a form readily taken in by plants and so is used as a natural fertiliser.

Inflorescence

Clusters of **flowers** on a **stalk** of a **plant**. A catkin is an example of an inflorescence. In many cases the flowers open in a pattern, beginning at the bottom and then moving to the top of the stalk. Bluebells have this type of inflorescence.

Insectivorous plant

(*See:* **Carnivorous plant**.)

Kingdom

One of the basic divisions of a **classification** of living things. There are five kingdoms: plants and animals are the largest. The three smaller kingdoms are Protista (such as **algae**, which have some similarities to both plants and animals), bacteria and the plant-like organisms called **fungi**.

▲ **Infloresence** – The flowers of the bottlebrush tree form large inflorescences to attract insects.

Lateral bud

A **bud** that forms between the **stem** and a **leaf stalk**. This bud can grow into a new stem, leaf, or **flower**. When people prune a **plant**, they prune to just above a lateral bud, knowing that the bud will then burst into growth.

Lateral root

A side or branch **root** leading off the main **taproot**.

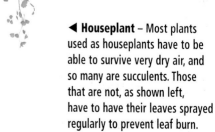

◄ **Houseplant** – Most plants used as houseplants have to be able to survive very dry air, and so many are succulents. Those that are not, as shown left, have to have their leaves sprayed regularly to prevent leaf burn.

Leaf, leaves

A leaf is a flat, blade-like growth from the **stem** of a **plant** (*see also:* **Node**). Leaves are actually part of the stem and they grow from **buds** along the side of the stem (*see:* **Lateral bud**). **Spines** are another kind of stem growth.

The **blade** of a leaf is attached to the main stem by a **stalk** called a **petiole**. The blade is supported by a natural 'scaffolding' called the **veins**. The veins also bring **minerals** and water to the leaf and carry food away to other parts of the plant. Veins spread out from the stalk (*see also:* **Vascular system**). Plants that **germinate** with two leaves (called **dicotyledons**) have veins that form a branching net, while those that **germinate** with one leaf (called **monocotyledons**) have only major veins, which tend to be parallel with one another.

A leaf may be a single blade – in which case it is called a simple leaf – or it may be made of many leaflets, in which case it is called a compound leaf. A leaf may have several lobes or parts, but still be a simple leaf (*see:* **Leaf types**).

Some leaves may be spines, while others may be small scales.

Leaves are green because the main purpose of the leaf is to manufacture food using minerals, water, air and sunlight (*see:* **Photosynthesis**). The active part of the leaf is the green substance called **chlorophyll**, which is found in all leaf **cells**.

The leaf has an outer protective surface coating. It forms a continuous sheet with the stem of the plant, is often waxy and does not let air or water through (*see:* **Cuticle**).

The centre of the leaf consists of soft cells in which up to a fifth of the bulk is chlorophyll. The chlorophyll absorbs light energy and uses it to split water into the two gases, hydrogen and oxygen. The

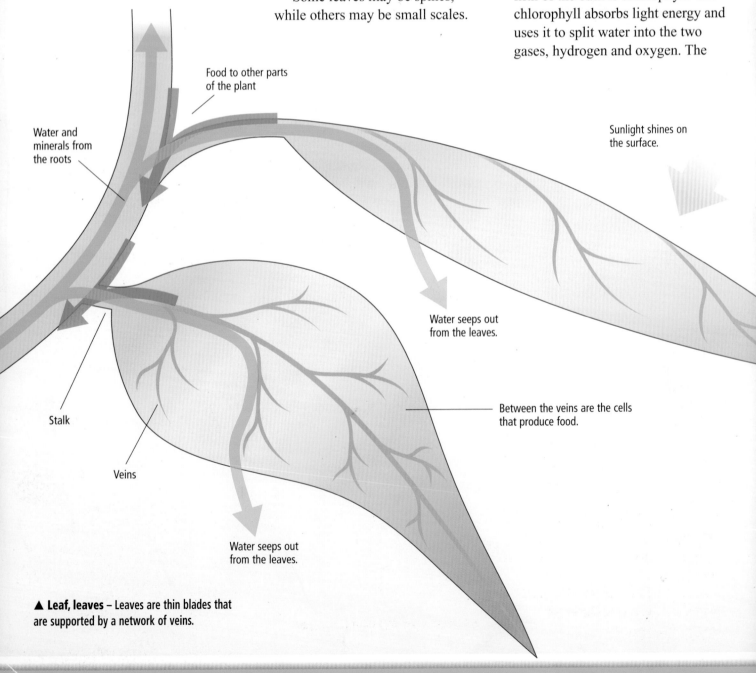

Food to other parts of the plant

Water and minerals from the roots

Sunlight shines on the surface.

Water seeps out from the leaves.

Stalk

Between the veins are the cells that produce food.

Veins

Water seeps out from the leaves.

▲ **Leaf, leaves** – Leaves are thin blades that are supported by a network of veins.

plant has no use for the oxygen, which is then allowed to escape to the air through tiny surface **pores** called **stomata**. At the same time, the pores allow carbon dioxide into the leaf, which is combined with the hydrogen to form **sugars** that can be used both to make new **tissues** and as a source of energy. (*See also:* **Respiration**.)

While the leaf is growing, chlorophyll – a green material – is the most common pigment and gives the leaves their green **colour**. However, in places with a cold autumn certain **deciduous trees** change leaf colour very dramatically, turning from green to bright yellow (aspens) or red (maples). This happens because the chlorophyll **pigment** breaks down and loses its colour, allowing the other pigments to show through. The other colours are made by carotene and xanthophyll (yellow) and anthocyanin and betacyanin (red).

Leaves are not intended to last long. They are at their most active and useful to the plant during their first year. In **evergreen** plants, on which leaves might last for two or three years, the older leaves contribute little to the plant growth.

Whether leaves fall off after the first growing season, or whether they survive for several years, they will eventually fall off. This happens when a plant triggers changes in its cells at the base of the **leaf stalk,** creating a zone of weaker cells. At the same time, most of the nourishment in the leaf seeps back into the stem. Eventually, the weight of the leaf causes the weak layer to fail and the leaf falls. A healing layer then forms over the wound and produces a **leaf scar**.

(*See also:* **Canopy**; **Life cycle**; **Vegetative growth**.)

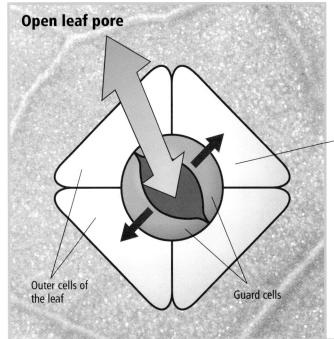

Open leaf pore

Outer cells of the leaf

Guard cells

◀ **Leaf pore** – This diagram shows the way in which the guard cells of a leaf pore open and close.

When the guard cells open, air and water vapour can move in and out of the leaf pore.

Leaf pore

The opening, usually on the underside of the **leaf**, through which a **plant** takes in carbon dioxide from the air and sends out water vapour and oxygen. The scientific name is **stoma**. (*See also:* **Guard cells**; **Hormones**; **Respiration**; **Succulent**; **Transpiration**; **Turgor movements**.)

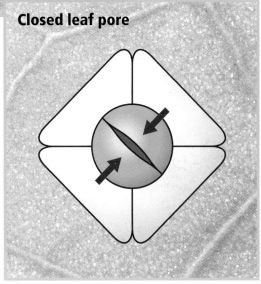

Closed leaf pore

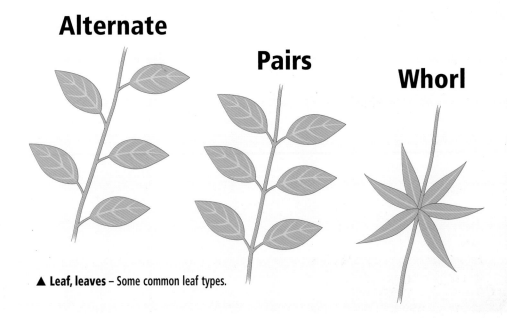

Alternate

Pairs

Whorl

▲ **Leaf, leaves** – Some common leaf types.

◀ **Leaf scar** – Leaf scars mark previous years' growth.

Leaf scar

Leaf scar

The mark left on a **twig** that shows where a **leaf** was once attached.

Leaf stalk

The **stalk** that attaches a **leaf** to a **stem** (also called petiole). (*See also:* **Node**.)

Legume, leguminous crop

Any **crop**, such as alfalfa or clover, that produces nodules on its **roots** that are rich in nitrogen. They act as a natural source of fertiliser, and legumes are often used in **crop rotation** with **cereal crops**.

▼ **Lichen** – Many kinds of fungi completely covering stones high in the Colorado Rockies.

Lichens

Very slow developing and flat plant-like forms that grow on bare rock and other surfaces. They are a combination of green **algae** and **fungi**. (*See also:* **Epiphyte**.)

Life cycle

The series of stages in the growth of a **plant** from its development as a **seed** until it has reproduced and died. Plants continue to grow throughout their lives, adding new **stems** and producing new **leaves** and **flowers**. This is quite different from animals, which grow to adulthood and then stop growing. For example, plants grow towards the light to get a better position for their leaves.

The life cycle begins when a **seed germinates**, or sprouts. Seeds are **dormant**, or inactive, when they are shed from a **fruit**, and so there has to be some mechanism to trigger them into action. It might be warmth, moisture, longer day length, or even fire.

Once germination has happened, the **root** grows and then the **shoot** develops. Both root and shoot grow at their tips, while **woody plants** also grow in the **cambium** layer just below the **bark**. Plants develop under the control of **hormones**, chemical messengers that make sure growth and other changes take place in a coordinated way.

The early stages of growth are called **vegetative**, when plants add to their roots, stems and put out new leaves. Later on, vegetative growth is replaced by **reproductive growth**. We normally see it as the formation of **buds**, then flowers and finally fruit.

As soon as the flower has been fertilised (*see:* **Pollination** and **Fertilisation**), it withers and plant has no use for the oxygen, which is then allowed to escape to the air through tiny surface **pores** called **stomata**. At the same time, the pores allow carbon dioxide into the leaf, which is combined with the hydrogen to form **sugars** that can be used both to make new **tissues** and as a source of energy. (*See also:* **Respiration**.)

While the leaf is growing, chlorophyll – a green material – is the most common pigment and gives the leaves their green **colour**. However, in places with a cold autumn certain **deciduous trees** change leaf colour very dramatically, turning from green to bright yellow (aspens) or red (maples). This happens because the chlorophyll **pigment** breaks down and loses its colour, allowing the other pigments to show through. The other colours are made by carotene and xanthophyll (yellow) and anthocyanin and betacyanin (red).

Leaves are not intended to last long. They are at their most active and useful to the plant during their first year. In **evergreen** plants, on which leaves might last for two or three years, the older leaves contribute little to the plant growth.

Whether leaves fall off after the first growing season, or whether they survive for several years, they will eventually fall off. This happens when a plant triggers changes in its cells at the base of the **leaf stalk**, creating a zone of weaker cells. At the same time, most of the nourishment in the leaf seeps back into the stem. Eventually, the weight of the leaf causes the weak layer to fail and the leaf falls. A healing layer then forms over the wound and produces a **leaf scar**.

(*See also:* **Canopy**; **Life cycle**; **Vegetative growth**.)

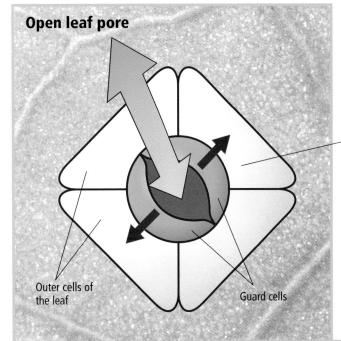

Open leaf pore

Outer cells of the leaf

Guard cells

◀ **Leaf pore** – This diagram shows the way in which the guard cells of a leaf pore open and close.

When the guard cells open, air and water vapour can move in and out of the leaf pore.

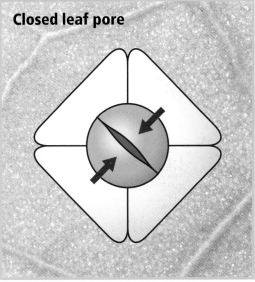

Closed leaf pore

Leaf pore

The opening, usually on the underside of the **leaf**, through which a **plant** takes in carbon dioxide from the air and sends out water vapour and oxygen. The scientific name is **stoma**. (*See also:* **Guard cells**; **Hormones**; **Respiration**; **Succulent**; **Transpiration**; **Turgor movements**.)

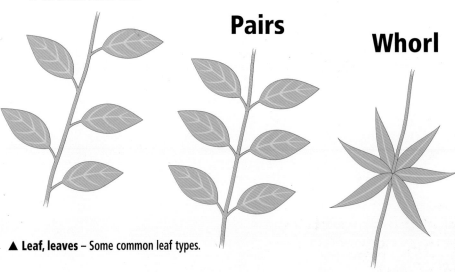

Alternate

Pairs

Whorl

▲ **Leaf, leaves** – Some common leaf types.

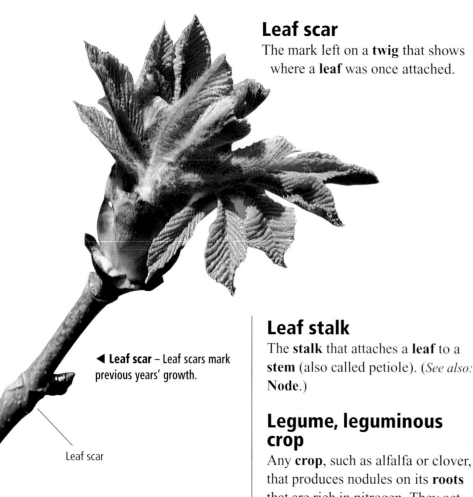

Leaf scar

The mark left on a **twig** that shows where a **leaf** was once attached.

◄ **Leaf scar** – Leaf scars mark previous years' growth.

Leaf scar

Leaf stalk

The **stalk** that attaches a **leaf** to a **stem** (also called petiole). (*See also:* **Node.**)

Legume, leguminous crop

Any **crop**, such as alfalfa or clover, that produces nodules on its **roots** that are rich in nitrogen. They act as a natural source of fertiliser, and legumes are often used in **crop rotation** with **cereal crops**.

▼ **Lichen** – Many kinds of fungi completely covering stones high in the Colorado Rockies.

Lichens

Very slow developing and flat plant-like forms that grow on bare rock and other surfaces. They are a combination of green **algae** and **fungi**. (*See also:* **Epiphyte**.)

Life cycle

The series of stages in the growth of a **plant** from its development as a **seed** until it has reproduced and died. Plants continue to grow throughout their lives, adding new **stems** and producing new **leaves** and **flowers**. This is quite different from animals, which grow to adulthood and then stop growing. For example, plants grow towards the light to get a better position for their leaves.

The life cycle begins when a **seed germinates**, or sprouts. Seeds are **dormant**, or inactive, when they are shed from a **fruit**, and so there has to be some mechanism to trigger them into action. It might be warmth, moisture, longer day length, or even fire.

Once germination has happened, the **root** grows and then the **shoot** develops. Both root and shoot grow at their tips, while **woody plants** also grow in the **cambium** layer just below the **bark**. Plants develop under the control of **hormones**, chemical messengers that make sure growth and other changes take place in a coordinated way.

The early stages of growth are called **vegetative**, when plants add to their roots, stems and put out new leaves. Later on, vegetative growth is replaced by **reproductive growth**. We normally see it as the formation of **buds**, then flowers and finally fruit.

As soon as the flower has been fertilised (*see:* **Pollination** and **Fertilisation**), it withers and

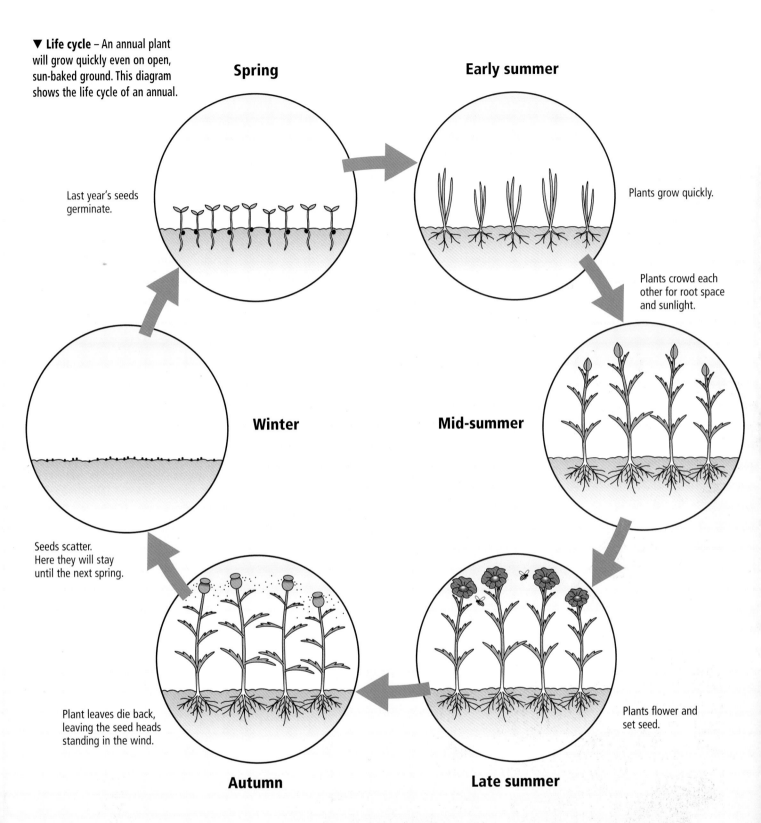

▼ **Life cycle** – An annual plant will grow quickly even on open, sun-baked ground. This diagram shows the life cycle of an annual.

Spring

Early summer

Last year's seeds germinate.

Plants grow quickly.

Plants crowd each other for root space and sunlight.

Winter

Mid-summer

Seeds scatter. Here they will stay until the next spring.

Plant leaves die back, leaving the seed heads standing in the wind.

Plants flower and set seed.

Autumn

Late summer

the fruit grows. The seeds develop inside the fruit.

Once the seeds are fully developed, they have to be scattered well clear of the parent plant. This is achieved by directly throwing them out of the seed head or letting the wind or animals carry them.

A plant may go through this cycle of growth and fruiting many times during its life. An oak, for example, may live for over a thousand years and make and scatter many thousands of **acorns** each year. Finally, when the plant has completed its life, it dies and

the **tissues** of the plant are decomposed by microbes and returned to the soil to provide nourishment for the next generation (*see:* **Decay, decaying**).

(*See also:* **Annual; Biennial; Ephemeral**.)

M

Mineral

In **botany**, an inorganic chemical element that is necessary for life. In this sense it is similar to the word **nutrient**, except that nutrients can be both organic and inorganic substances. A **plant** takes in dissolved minerals through its **roots** in the water it sucks up from the soil. Such minerals include calcium, nitrogen and potassium. (*See also:* **Xylem**.)

Monocotyledon

A **flowering plant** that has one **leaf** in its **seed**. (*See also:* **Stem** and **Vein**.)

Moss

A small, flowerless green **plant** that lacks true **roots**, growing in low carpets or rounded cushions in damp habitats. It reproduces by means of **spores** released from capsules on stalks.

Many small plants popularly called mosses are **algae**, **lichen**, or **herbs**. The green 'mossy' covering on the north side of a **tree** is an algae, for example, and club moss is an evergreen herb.

▶ **Moss** – Stalked capsules rising above a moss on a wall.

▶ **Nectar** – A monarch butterfly feeding on the nectar of a lantana plant, Guatemala.

N

Native

A **plant** or animal that lives naturally in a particular **habitat** (*see also:* **Weed**), as opposed to one that has been introduced from another place (*see:* **Exotic plant**).

Nectar

A sweet, sticky substance produced by **flowers** (as well as some **stems** and **leaves**), and that attracts animals such as insects, bats and humming-birds. When the animals enter a flower

to reach the nectar, they brush against **pollen** held on **stamens** inside the flower and in this way transfer pollen from one **plant** to another. Nectar thus aids **pollination**.

(*See also:* **Anther** and **Nectary**.)

Nectary

The part of a **flower** that produces a sugary liquid – **nectar** – on which animals feed.

Needle

A long, narrow, rod-like **leaf** often found on **conifers**.

▲ **Needle** – Needles are important in helping a conifer stand up to winter snow and drought and be able to absorb sunlight quickly in spring.

Node

The place where the **leaves** of a **plant** are attached to the **stem**. (*See also:* **Stipule**.)

Nucleus

The inside part of the **cell** that controls its growth, development and activities.

Nut (part of a plant)

A dry, hard **fruit** with a tough, woody shell that does not easily split open. Chestnuts and **acorns** are nuts.

Many nut-like fruits are not strictly nuts. A peanut, for example, is a legume (*see:* **Leguminous crop**) and a coconut is a **drupe**. The brazil nut is a **seed** in biological terms.

Nut (food)

A general term referring to most edible hard-shelled **fruits**, nodules, or **seeds** of a **plant**. Among the most widely eaten nuts are brazil nuts, cashews, peanuts and almonds. All are rich in **oil** and fat.

▶ **Nut** – Hazelnut ripening.

Nutrient

A substance needed by an organism for healthy growth. Nutrients can be **minerals** or substances produced by **plants** or animals.

Plants can get all of their nourishment from minerals in the soil and water and from carbon dioxide in the air. (*See also:* **Humus**; **Osmosis**; **Vascular system**.)

There are nine essential elements that a plant needs in large amounts: carbon (C), hydrogen (H), oxygen (O), nitrogen (N), potassium (K), calcium (Ca), magnesium (Mg), phosphorus (P) and sulphur (S). Carbon, hydrogen, oxygen and nitrogen make up 96% of the weight of plants (excluding water).

There are seven more essential elements needed in small amounts: iron (Fe), chlorine (Cl), manganese (Mn), boron (B), copper (Cu), molybdenum (Mo) and zinc (Zn).

The elements needed in small amounts are often those that control the rate of growth of the plant.

Plants get these elements as compounds that they must break down to get what they need. For example, nitrogen occurs combined with oxygen as nitrate (NO_3), carbon comes from carbon dioxide (CO_2) and hydrogen comes as water (H_2O.)

Carbon dioxide provides all the carbon and two-thirds of the oxygen that a plant needs. Water, sucked from the soil by **roots**, provides a third of the oxygen and most of the hydrogen plants need. The soil also provides all of the other elements in soluble form.

When fertiliser is applied to a garden or field, it usually contains the nutrients mentioned above. Nitrogen is important for fleshy growth and is applied to plants to make them leafier. Potassium makes plants **flower** and produce **seeds** more effectively. (*See also:* **Crop rotation**.)

O

Oil

Fat and oil are a very concentrated source of energy. **Plants** produce both of them and use them to store energy in places where space is in short supply, for example, in **seeds**. All seeds contain oil, but some seeds (for example, sunflower) are especially rich in it. People take the oil from them for cooking and other processes. (*See also:* **Rubber**.)

▲ **Oil** – This is a close-up of clusters of palm oil nuts waiting for processing.

▼ **Oil** – Jets of pungent smelling, oily liquid are produced when this fruit is squeezed. The ancient Maya of Central America used this as their incense.

▲ **Parasitic plant** – A mistletoe growing on the branch of an apple tree.

Osmosis

A process that acts like a filter, allowing the solvent in a solution to pass through, but not the materials dissolved in it. It is important in the way **plants** work. Inside the **roots**, for example, there is a much higher concentration of salt than in the surrounding soil water. The water in the soil flows into the root to make the water in the root less salty (and make the saltiness the same as that in the water in the soil). As a result, water from the soil flows into the root. Water always moves from a less salty to a more salty solution, so water rarely flows out of the roots. Osmosis therefore allows plants to take up water from the surrounding soil.

Ovary

The part of the **flower** at the base of the **pistil**, where the **seeds** form in **flowering plants**. (*See also:* **Ovule**.)

Ovule

The structure in the **ovary** that contains the female sex **cell**, or egg cell. It is an immature **seed**.

P

Parasitic plant

Plants that grow on other plants and extract the nourishment they need from their host. One of the most well-known parasitic plants is mistletoe. It feeds on **trees** by sending **roots** into the water- and food-carrying tubes in the **stem** (*see:* **Vascular system**). The **branches** of a tree on which mistletoe is growing may lose so much of their nourishment that they die.

Perennial

A **plant** that lives for many years. **Shrubs** and **trees** are all perennials, but so are plants of more modest size. Where conditions are harsh, such as high up on mountains or in the cold tundra lands close to ice caps, all of the plants are perennials,

growing by just a small amount each year. All of the plants in a equatorial **rainforest** are also perennials because here there are no seasons for **annuals** to thrive. (*See also:* **Adaptation, adapt; Alpine; Herbaceous plants**.)

Petal

One of a circle of large, coloured blades in a **flower**. A petal is, in fact, a modified leaf that surrounds the male and female parts of a **plant**. The petals are often brightly coloured and sometimes scented so that they act like flags, making sure the flower is easily spotted by **pollinating** animals. (*See also:* **Colour; Corolla; Sepal**.)

Petiole

(*See:* **Leaf stalk**.)

Phloem

A special group of tubes inside a **plant stem** that carry food in the form of dissolved **sugars** from the **leaves** to other parts of the plant (compare with **xylem**). (*See also:* **Vascular system**.)

▲ **Photosynthesis** – Beech leaves spread horizontally to absorb the strongest sunlight.

Photosynthesis

The process in which the green **chlorophyll** in a **plant** uses the energy in sunlight to make food and oxygen from water (hydrogen and oxygen) and carbon dioxide.

Photosynthesis produces a **sugar** called glucose that can be broken down and used for energy in the form of a sugar called sucrose, or changed into **starch** and stored for later use. Starch is stored in **roots**, **stems** and **seeds**. Photosynthesis takes place at the same time as **respiration**.

(*See also:* **Leaf, leaves.**)

SUNLIGHT

WATER and MINERALS

from the roots

Water and minerals travel up the roots through the water tubes in the stem, leaf stalk and veins.

+

CARBON DIOXIDE

from the surrounding air

All plants contain an element called carbon. Carbon is found as a gas called carbon dioxide, which is part of the air.

...using energy from sunlight to produce...

Energy is trapped by chlorophyll in the cells of the leaf.

▲ **Photosynthesis** – Photosynthesis is the name of the process used by plants to make new cells and tissues, and to obtain energy for living.

◀ **Pigment** – Red oak leaves in the autumn. The chlorophyll pigment has decomposed.

Pigment

A chemical that appears coloured in light. Pigments such as **chlorophyll** give **plants** a green **colour**. In **deciduous** trees the chlorophyll pigment decomposes just before the **leaves** fall off, and this allows the colours of the remaining pigments to show through as yellows, browns and reds.

Pistil

The bottle-shaped, **seed**-bearing structure at the centre of the **flower**. It is made of one or more **carpels**. The parts of the pistil are called the **ovary**, **stigma** and **style**. (*See also:* **Fertilisation**.)

Plant

One of the main groups of living things. There are about 300,000 different **species** of plants. Plants get their food and energy by making use of sunlight (a process called **photosynthesis**). The plant uses sunlight to produce chemical energy (in the form of **sugars**) from water, **minerals** and carbon dioxide. Plants have stiff **cell** walls

that prevent their limbs and leaves from being as flexible as many other living things. They continue to grow throughout their entire life and do not have a fixed size and shape (**form**). They do not seem to have a nervous system.

Because there are so many kinds of plants, simple definitions will not include all of them. For example, not all plants are green or have **leaves** and not all plants use sunlight to make food (for example, **parasitic plants** like orchids).

Plants were the earliest living things and have existed for billions of years. At first they lived only in oceans, but then they moved onto land. As a result, they have evolved into many shapes and sizes (*see:* **Evolution, plant**). The smallest, like duckweeds, are only a few millimetres across, while the largest plants on Earth, the giant sequoias of California, are over 90m tall.

Plants are essential for all other life on Earth. Only plants can get energy from the Sun. Most animals get all the energy they need from eating plants. Plant-eating animals take energy from the **sugars** stored in plant leaves. Other animals, including humans, use the more nutritious parts of a plant, including the **roots** and **seeds**.

Plants also release oxygen as part of their process of photosynthesis. Without this oxygen, life on Earth would be impossible for animals. Plants that live on land are very different from plants that live

in water, because those in the water do not need to protect themselves from drying out, nor do they need to find ways of holding themselves up. Plants on land all have a waxy covering to prevent loss of water, and they reproduce by using **pollen**. None of these features are found in water plants.

Plants are important in all aspects of human lives, not just because they provide oxygen and food, but also because they can be made into **wood**, **oil**, **rubber**, **fibres**, medicines, insecticides and fuels. Plants also protect the environment, their roots holding the soil in place and their leaves preventing rain from spattering directly onto the soil. Their roots help break up the soil and so make it easier for water to soak in. By **transpiring**, they take water from the soil and so make room for more rainfall. In these ways plants help reduce flooding. By making it easier for rainwater to soak into the soil, plants also allow the soil to provide a natural filter for water and so help maintain the cleanliness of river water. Conserving plants is therefore as important to us as it is to the plants, for without them we could not survive.

(*For plant types see:* **Alpine**; **Angiosperm**; **Annual**; **Aquatic**; **Biennial**; **Cactus**; **Carnivorous**; **Cereal**; **Climbing plants**; **Citrus**; **Crop**; **Cultivated**; **Deciduous**; **Dicotyledons**; **Epiphyte**; **Evergreen**; **Exotic**; **Fern**; **Foliage plants**; **Flowering plant**; **Gymnosperm**; **Herbaceous**; **Houseplant**; **Monocotyledons**; **Native**; **Perennial**; **Seed plants**; **Shrub**; **Succulent**; **Vascular plants**; **Weed**.)

OXYGEN

which is released into the surrounding air

Air contains oxygen, which the plant does not need. It is released through the leaf pores.

+

TISSUES

which the plant needs to grow

Pollen

Yellow-coloured grains that are produced by the male parts of a **flower**. Pollen contains the male sex **cells**. (*See also:* **Anther**; **Cone**; **Pollination, pollinate**.)

Pollination, pollinate

The transfer of **pollen** between the male parts of one **flower** and the female parts of another flower.

During pollination, pollen is carried from its source on the (male) **anther** of one flower to the sticky surface of the (female) **stigma** in another; or for **cone**-bearing **plants**, from the male cone to the female cone.

There are two kinds of pollination. Those plants that use **wind pollination** have small flowers and disperse huge volumes of pollen into the air. Those plants that use **insect pollination** have brightly coloured flowers and attract insects by producing nectar.

Pollination is the first stage of **fertilisation**.

(*See also:* **Cross-pollination**; **Life cycle**; **Nectar**; **Propagate**; **Reproduction**; **Self-pollination**.)

Pollen carried by the wind.

Male hazel flowers called catkins produce pollen.

Female hazel flowers are tiny but have a sticky surface to their stigma to catch the pollen floating in the wind.

◀▲ **Pollination** – The common hazel is pollinated by the wind.

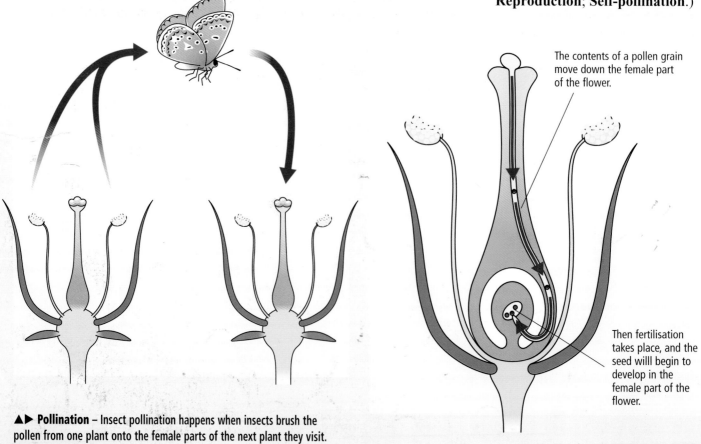

The contents of a pollen grain move down the female part of the flower.

Then fertilisation takes place, and the seed will begin to develop in the female part of the flower.

▲▶ **Pollination** – Insect pollination happens when insects brush the pollen from one plant onto the female parts of the next plant they visit.

Pore

A very small, round opening, often on the underside of a **plant leaf**. (Also called a **leaf pore** or **stoma**.)

Prop root

(*See:* **Adventitious root**.)

Propagate

A general word meaning to reproduce. It can occur by the transfer of **pollen** (*see:* **Pollination**) or by sending out side **stems** above ground (**runners**) or below ground (**rhizomes**). (*See also:* **Cutting**; **Grafting**; **Reproduction**.)

Protista

(*See:* **Algae**.)

R

Rainforest

A **community** of **plants** that grows in an area where rainfall occurs throughout much of the year. In the areas near the equator, rainforests are called tropical or equatorial (*See also:* **Adaptation, adapt**; **Canopy**; **Evergreen**.)

Reproduction

The process by which all living things produce more of their own kind. There are two basic types of plant reproduction. One uses male and female 'parents', and the other needs only one 'parent'. Single-parent reproduction produces offspring that are identical to the lone parent. **Spores**, **rhizomes**, **runners**, **bulbs** and **tubers** are all produced this way. This kind of reproduction allows no opportunity for change through evolution. However, it is a fast way of producing new plants.

Two-parent reproduction combines male sex **cells** of one plant with female sex cells of another plant. This happens through the transfer of **pollen**. **Pollination** produces new plants relatively slowly, but it produces new plants that will be slightly different from the parents. This kind of reproduction allows the plant to evolve and change.

Many of the successful plants we called **weeds** reproduce by rhizomes and runners as well as through pollen.

Reproductive growth

The stage in the **life cycle** of a **plant** when it makes **buds**, **flowers** and **fruit**. (*See also:* **Vegetative growth**.)

Resin

A sticky substance produced by some **plants** when they are injured. Many resins are either transparent, amber or brown.

Pines and firs are trees whose **bark** leaks large quantities of resin as a result of an injury, such as when a **branch** becomes broken. The resin hardens in air and seals the wound. By cutting into the bark, trees can be made to produce resin that can be collected and used for varnishes and lacquers. Resin is not the same as **sap**.

(*See also:* **Rubber**.)

Respiration

The way a **plant** breathes. It does this by exchanging gases through the tiny holes called **pores**, or **stomata**, on the underside of the **leaves**. A plant takes up carbon dioxide through the pores and sends out waste gases, which include oxygen.

Respiration, **transpiration** and **photosynthesis** take place at the same time. The energy from sunlight makes it possible for the plant to take in the gases it needs and expel those it does not need.

Rhizome

An underground **stem**. It often contains joints from which **roots** and new **stems** can appear.

By using rhizomes, **plants** can spread by single-parent **reproduction**. All of the plants formed from rhizomes are the same as the parent. They are **clones**. Many kinds of grasses, **ferns** and forest **herbs** extend themselves (**propagate**) by rhizomes.

▼ **Rhizome** – This is a rhizome of an iris. The iris is able to store large amounts of food in this swollen stem.

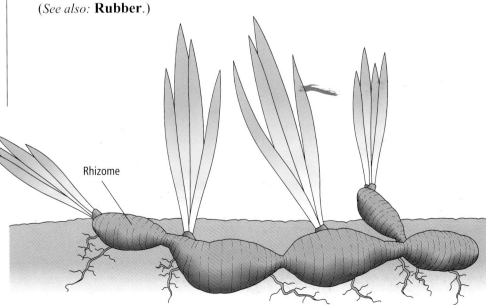

Rhizome

Root

Root

The part of a **plant** that is normally found underground. The purposes of a root are to anchor the plant in the ground and to suck up water and dissolved **minerals** and **nutrients** from the soil and send them to the **stem** and **leaves** (*see:* **Xylem**).

Roots also store food (as seen clearly, for example, in a carrot) (*see:* **Starch**).

Many underground parts of a plant that look like roots are, in fact, special parts of the stem. Such stem parts are called **bulbs**, **tubers** and **corms**. A root can be distinguished from a stem because it has branches that come directly from other roots rather than from **buds**.

When a **seed germinates**, the first part of the plant to emerge is the root. It grows downwards into the soil, anchoring the **seedling** and collecting water and nutrients. In many cases it becomes a long root called a **taproot**. Branches then form from it.

Plants such as grasses have a **fibrous root** system with no taproot. Many fibrous roots grow directly from the base of the stem, each branching in turn (*see also:* **Hormones**).

Roots grow from their ends. At the very end of the root is a protective skin or root cap. Roots also grow tiny hairs – effectively rootlets – that greatly add to the surface area of the root and make it easier for the root to suck up water from between soil particles.

Roots add to the size of **woody** plants by producing a bark-like covering.

Some roots form from the stem above ground. **Buttress roots** are an example of this. Other roots begin high up on a plant and then dangle in the air. They are called **aerial roots**.

▼ **Roots** – Roots are of two kinds: fibrous roots and taproots. The plant on the left has a taproot as well as fibrous roots. The carrot on the right has only a taproot.

Side roots spread out in search of water and nutrients, and form a sturdy support in the soil.

Some plants only have fibrous roots.

Water and minerals pass through the root hairs into larger passageways to reach other parts of the plant where they are needed for nourishment.

The taproot burrows down into the soil to anchor the plant and to find water during drought.

Water between soil particles contains dissolved minerals. The minerals are the nourishment the plant needs.

The very end of each root has a tough skin that protects it as it burrows its way through the soil.

Many more roots develop from underground stems. They are the roots that allow a plant to reproduce without seeds (*see:* **Rhizome** and **Runner**). Many grasses spread by this means.

(*See also:* **Aerial root**; **Anchor root**; **Fibre**; **Lateral root**; **Life cycle**; **Osmosis**.)

Root crop

A **crop** grown for its large **roots** (for example, turnips and carrots). (*See also:* **Vegetable**.)

38

Rubber

Made from solids that are suspended in a milky fluid, called latex, found in the inner part of the **bark** of tropical and subtropical **trees** and **shrubs** and also in **plants** like poppies. Latex consists of a mixture of **oils**, **resins** and waxes suspended in a watery liquid.

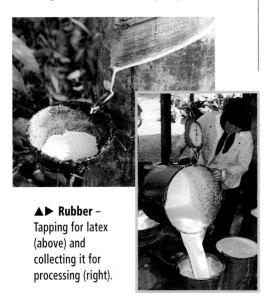

▲▶ **Rubber –** Tapping for latex (above) and collecting it for processing (right).

Runner

A side stem from the main **stem** that grows horizontally above the surface of the ground. Runners have joints from which **roots** grow if they touch the ground. Common **houseplants**, such as the spider plant, have runners that produce roots and stems from joints even while still in the air. Plants such as blackberry and buttercup **propagate** by runners.

All plants produced from runners are **clones** of the parent plant.

▶ **Seasonal rings –** Tree rings show changes in growth through the seasons – fast growth (light coloured) in spring and slower growth (dark coloured) in the summer. There is no growth in the winter.

The dead wood in the centre hardens, making the stem stronger.

S

Sap

The watery fluid found in **plants**. There are two kinds of sap: that stored in the **cells** and that which is free to flow through the plant. The main tubes running through the **stems** and **leaves** have two kinds of sap. **Xylem** sap carries water and dissolved **minerals** from the roots to the leaves. The water from this sap is then lost through the **leaf pores**, while the dissolved materials are used to build new **tissues**. **Phloem** sap carries sugar from leaves to other parts of the plant during the summer.

▼ **Runners –** Buttercups are common plants that have runners.

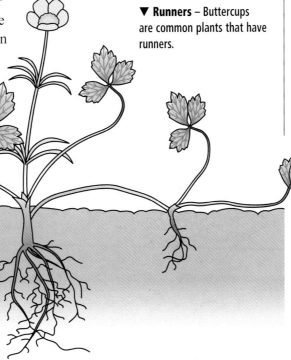

The outer ring is the 'live' and growing part of the tree, adding a new layer each year.

The surface is covered by a protective 'skin' of bark.

Seasonal rings

The rings seen when a **tree trunk** is cut. They show the history of growth of the tree in a place where there is a seasonal climate.

During the growing season the rate of growth changes, being fastest in spring when moisture is abundant and slower in summer when there is less moisture left in the soil. The growth in a year makes up a ring, with large **cells** on the inside and smaller cells on the outside. The following year sees a new spurt of spring growth that begins on the outside of the small cells of the previous summer. This junction is usually very easy to spot.

Tree rings are not found on trees from regions without regular seasonal change (for example, tropical **rainforest** trees).

Annual rings vary in thickness from less than 1mm to more than 1cm. The thickness in any year depends on the kind of tree, how old it is and the weather in spring and summer. The age of a tree can be found by counting its annual rings.

Seed

An immature **plant**, together with a supply of food (*see:* **Starch and Oil**), protected by a hard coating.

Seeds of **flowering plants** form at the base of a **flower** in the **ovary**. As the seed matures, the base of the flower forms a swollen, rounded shape called a **fruit**. A fruit does not have to be fleshy.

In the case of **conifers**, the seeds are exposed in a **cone** rather than being protected in a fruit.

Most seeds are small. If they are very small, there is no room inside the seed for a food supply. These seeds, like those of the orchid, have to get their food supply from other plants. The biggest seeds (such as coconut) may weigh over 20kg and contain a large food supply.

A seed will only **germinate** if the conditions are right. The trigger may be light, warmth, moisture, day length, or even fire. To germinate, both water and oxygen must be able to get through the hard outer covering of the seed. Some seeds can survive without

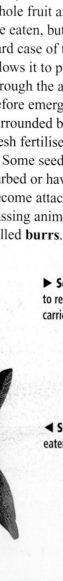

germinating for hundreds of years, while others can only germinate within their first week.

Flowering plants have many different ways of scattering their seeds. Some let the wind carry them, others use animals and some even use water. The seeds carried on the wind often have some form of parachute or sling, enabling them to drift away from their parent. Very small seeds can be carried quite long distances in a strong wind.

Seeds that are a source of food are often enclosed in a fleshy fruit. The whole fruit and seed are eaten, but the hard case of the seed allows it to pass right through the animal before emerging, surrounded by its own fresh fertiliser.

Some seeds and fruits are barbed or have hooks that easily become attached to the coats of passing animals. These fruits are called **burrs**.

A few plants can fire their seeds into the air with natural catapults.
(*See also:* **Life cycle** and **Seed plants**.)

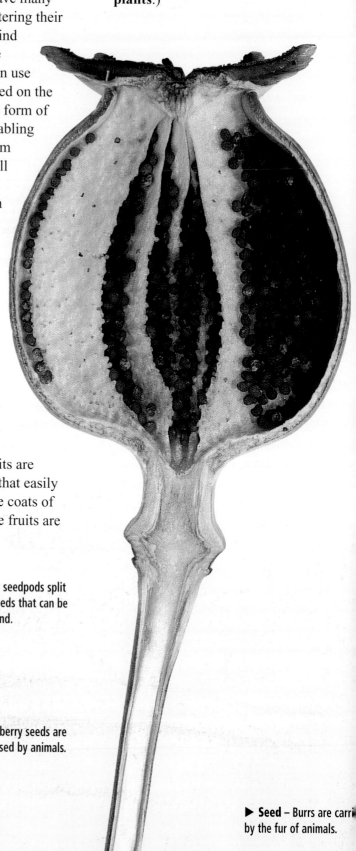

▶ **Seed** – Poppy seedpods split to release tiny seeds that can be carried by the wind.

◀ **Seed** – Strawberry seeds are eaten and dispersed by animals.

▶ **Seed** – Burrs are carri by the fur of animals.

◄ **Seed** – Dandelion seeds contain their own parachutes.

Seed plants

There are two groups of **plants** that bear **seeds**: the **gymnosperms** (such as **conifers**) and **angiosperms** (**flowering plants**). Seed plants differ from **spore** plants like **ferns** in the way they reproduce. Seed plants have evolved further than ferns and have more complicated ways of producing offspring, involving the transfer of **pollen** (*see:* **Pollination**). Seeds contain and protect a new plant and are much more able to survive than spores. These features have enabled seed plants to spread to a greater variety of **habitats** than ferns.

Seedling

A name for a **plant** between the time it **germinates** and when it becomes totally independent of the food stored in the **seed**. (*See also:* **Shoot**.)

◄ **Seed** – Maple seeds act as propeller blades as they descend.

▼ **Seedling** – Many seedlings will begin to sprout close together. Only the strongest will survive.

Self-pollination

A process of **pollination** in which **pollen** from within a **flower** reaches the female part of the same flower. Self-pollinating flowers often pollinate themselves before the flower even opens. This process produces **seeds** that are exact copies of the parent plants (**clones**). It has the same effect as sending out **runners** or **rhizomes** and is a fast way of increasing the plant population. (Compare this to **cross-pollination**.)

Sepal

One of the outermost circle of modified leaves that once protected the **bud**, but later surround and support the **petals**. They are usually small and green. (*See also:* **Calyx**.)

Shoot

Technically, the whole of the **plant** above the ground. The shoot consists of **stem** and **leaves**. Also used in a more general way to refer to the part of a **seedling** that emerges from the ground. (*See also:* **Fibre**; **Hormones**; **Life cycle**.)

Shrub

A **woody perennial plant** with many **stems** and usually less than 3m tall. (*See also:* **Bush**.)

Softwood

The name given to **wood** primarily from **coniferous trees** such as pine, fir and spruce. Softwoods are not necessarily softer than **hardwoods**. The difference lies in the way in which the **cells** and **fibres** of the trees form. The conifer wood is made mainly from a single type of cell, which carries sap and supports the **tree**. Conifers also tend to grow more quickly than hardwoods, so their cells are less compact, and the walls are softer than a hardwood tree.

▶ **Stem** – These are the stems (trunks) of the world's biggest plants – the giant redwoods.

Species

A group of similar-looking **plants** that can breed with one another and usually live in the same kind of **habitat**. (*See also:* **Genus** and **Kingdom**.)

Spine

A protective part of a **stem** or **leaf**. It is a hardened piece of stem that often forms into a needle-sharp spike. (*See also:* **Cactus, cacti**.)

Spore

The primitive 'seed' of some **plants** such as **ferns**, mosses and **fungi**. It is very small, carried by the wind, and is often very resistant to **decay** and may lie **dormant** for many years. Spores are a way of reproducing without transferring **pollen**. Spores are often released from sacs on the underside of **leaves**.

Stalk

On small **plants** such as **annuals**, the term used for the main **stem**. Stalks also connect **leaves** (*see:* **Leaf stalk**) and **fruit** to **branches** of larger plants.

Stamen

The male part of the **flower**, made from the sac-like **anther** and the long, thin **filament** that supports it.

Starch

A type of **carbohydrate** that is the main way in which **plants** store food (**sugars**). When it is needed, it is converted back to sugars, which can then be carried around the plant dissolved in water. Starch is stored in stems, roots and seeds. (*See also:* **Photosynthesis** and **Tuber**.)

Stem

The main vertical part of a **plant** (*see also:* **Stalk**). **Branches** and **leaves** form from the stem. In a **tree** the stem is called a **trunk**.

  Rhizomes are horizontally growing underground stems. They allow a plant to **propagate** without **pollen**. They also store food (*see:* **Starch**). **Tubers** (such as potatoes) are thick rhizomes. **Corms** are short, vertical underground stems surrounded by scale leaves (a crocus 'bulb' is

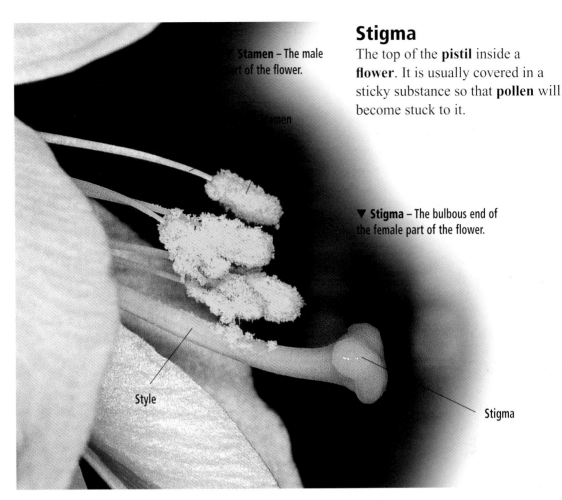

Stamen – The male part of the flower.

Style

Stigma

▼ **Stigma** – The bulbous end of the female part of the flower.

▲ **Style** – The centre of the female part of the flower.

Stigma

The top of the **pistil** inside a **flower**. It is usually covered in a sticky substance so that **pollen** will become stuck to it.

Stipule

Tiny leaflets that grow where the main **leaf** is attached to the **stem** (*see:* **Node**).

Stolon

A modified stem that runs across the surface of the ground (*see:* **Runner**).

Stoma/stomata

The scientific name for the **pores** in plant **leaves** that a **plant** uses to take in air and expel water and oxygen. (*See also:* **Guard cells; Leaf pore; Respiration; Succulent; Transpiration; Turgor movements.**)

Style

The centre of the female part of the **flower**. It connects the **seed-**producing **ovary** to the **pollen-**receiving **stigma** and is part of the **pistil**.

◀ **Stem** – Asparagus stems.

a corm). **Bulbs** have a short, vertical stem with thick, fleshy leaves (as in narcissus). **Runners** are surface stems that stretch out across the ground. They can produce new plants along their lengths.

Herbaceous plants do not have **bark**.

In 'two-leaf' plants (**dicotyledons**) woody stems form as an outer layer of dead, thick-walled **cells** called **cork**. **Woody plants** increase the thickness of their bark each year, as can be seen in their **seasonal rings**.

'One-leaf' plants (**monocotyledons**) do not grow in this way and so do not become woody.

(*See also:* **Climbing plants; Hormones; Turgor; Vascular system; Vegetative growth.**)

Succulent

A **plant** with fleshy, thick **leaves** and a **stem adapted** to conserving water. **Cacti** are examples of succulents. They store water only in the stem and have no leaves. Agaves are succulents that store water mainly in their leaves.

Most succulents have **roots** adapted to get the most water from dry conditions, either by spreading a network of fine, **fibrous roots** close to the surface, or by sending a **taproot** many metres deep into the soil.

In succulent plants the **leaf pores**, or **stomata**, are closed during the hot day and open at night. In this way they keep down the amount of water lost while the pores are open to allow air in. Succulents take in the carbon dioxide they need from the air at night, so they cannot break it down using **photosynthesis** in the same way as other plants can. Instead, they have a special mechanism that stores the carbon dioxide until the following day, when sunlight can again power photosynthesis.

Sugar

The general name for the substance produced by a **plant** during **photosynthesis**. Photosynthesis produces a compound called glucose. It is a sugar that can be converted into two more forms: sucrose, which dissolves and can be carried around the plant for food and energy and **starch**, which does not dissolve easily and which can be used as a source of stored food and energy. Sugars and starches are known as **carbohydrates** because they contain carbon, hydrogen and oxygen. (*See also:* **Phloem**.)

▶ **Thorn** – These vicious thorns belong to an African acacia.

T

Taproot

The large central **root** of some **plants** that is used to anchor the plant and to bring moisture to it. All plants sprout using a taproot, although in some cases the taproot does not grow and, instead, a mass of **fibrous roots** forms.

Taproots often store food and may become swollen in some plants, for example, in a carrot. (*See also:* **Anchor root** and **Lateral root**.)

Tendril

A part of a **leaf** or **stem** that has been modified into a whip-like shape that is used to attach the **plant** to a support. Tendrils are particularly common among **vines**. Tendrils have **cells** on their surface that are sensitive to touch. When the tendril touches something, these cells stop the tendril from stretching out and instead make it curl around in a direction facing the point of touch. In this way tendrils curl around a surface (often the stem or branch of another plant)

and use it for support. (*See also:* **Turgor movements**.)

Once a tendril has been in contact with a support for long enough, it begins to harden and become stronger. In this way it changes to a form that is more able to support the plant.

Some tendrils flatten out when they reach a support and exude a glue that allows them to stick to a surface even if they cannot wrap around it.

(*See:* **Adventitious roots** for an alternative way of providing support for **climbing plants**.)

Terminal bud

The **bud** at the tip of the **shoot**.

Thorn

A curved, sharp **spine** that is a special development of a **stem**. Thorns are part of the **defences** of some **plants**.

Tissue

The material from which **plants** are made. Each kind of tissue is made of one kind of **cell**. New tissues are made at the tips of the **shoots** and **roots**. (*See also:* **Carbohydrate**.)

▶ **Turgor movements** – When a finger touches the leaves of this sensitive plant, the leaves immediately turn down.

Transpiration

The way in which a **plant** sends out water through the tiny holes called **pores**, or **stomata**, on the underside of the **leaves** (*see:* **Leaf pores**).

Plants need to take up water (and the **nutrients** the water contains) through their **roots**. This is done, in part, by losing water through their leaves. As water is lost in the leaves, it creates a suction in the roots, which causes water to flow into the roots from the soil.

Transpiration happens at the same time, and through the same pores, as **respiration**. The plant loses water as a gas – water vapour.

Tree

A **perennial woody plant** that has a single main **trunk** and grows taller than about 4m to 5m.

Trunk

The large, woody **stem** of a **tree**.

Tuber

The short, swollen, underground **stem** of a **plant** in which food is stored in the form of **starch**. It is the resting stage of some plants. Tubers contain small growth points that can develop into new plants. A potato plant has tubers. Some people also use the term for fleshy **roots** and stems that look like tubers.

Turgor

Rigidity due to the pressure of water inside the **plant**. When water is removed, the plants lose turgor and **wilt**.

Turgor movements

The rapid movements of a **plant**, such as the snapping shut of a Venus fly trap, the closing of a **flower** at night, the wrapping of **tendrils** around a support, and the opening and closing of **leaf**

Twig

The small ends of a **branch**. Twigs are the **woody** growth of a previous season.

V

Vascular plants

Plants in which water and food are conducted through a network of fine tubes called **veins**. Scientists refer to veins as vascular bundles. (*See also:* **Vascular system**.)

Vascular system

A network of tubes and supporting **fibres** (**veins**) that allow **plants** to transport food and water between **leaves**, **stem** and **root**. There are two sets of tubes: one conducts water and **nutrients** from roots

pores. These movements happen because specialised **cells** quickly lose or gain water. Because some cells swell while others shrink, the positions of **petals** and **leaves** change, thus causing them to open and close.

to leaves (called **xylem**), and the other carries dissolved foods from the leaves to all parts of the plant (called **phloem**). Plants that do not have these tubes are called non-vascular plants. On land only the smallest plants fit this category. Many sea plants are non-vascular.

Because it is important not to let water seep away, the leaves and stems of vascular plants are coated in a waxy substance that does not easily let water or air through (*see:* **Cuticle**). However, plants need air and they need to get rid of surplus water. They do this through tiny holes known as **leaf pores** or **stomata**. These pores can be opened and closed to control the amount of air let in and water let out (*see:* **Transpiration**).

Vegetable

The edible part of an **herbaceous plant** – either **roots**, **stems**, **leaves**, **flowers** or **fruit**.

The type of vegetable group that a plant falls into depends on which part is used for food.

Root vegetables are those in which the root is the main source of food. They include beetroots, carrots and parsnips.

Stem vegetables are those in which the stem is eaten. They include asparagus.

Vegetables that belong to the swollen stem (**tuber**) group include potatoes.

Leaf and **leaf stalk** vegetables are those in which the leaf or the leaf stalk is eaten. They include Brussels sprouts, cabbage, celery, lettuce and rhubarb.

Bulb vegetables include garlic, leeks and onions.

Flower-head vegetables include broccoli and cauliflower.

Some fruits are also commonly thought of as vegetables. They include beans, cucumbers, sweetcorn and tomatoes.

Vegetables contain no **carbohydrates** and very little protein or fat, but they are often a rich source of **minerals**, such as calcium and iron, and vitamins A and C.

Vegetative growth

The stage in the **life cycle** of a **plant** when it grows new **roots**, **stems** and **leaves** (but no **flowers**). (*See also:* **Reproductive growth**.)

Vein

Long, thin supporting 'scaffolding' in a **leaf** that also carries water and food between the leaf and the **stem**. Veins are made from **fibres** and tubes. (*See also:* **Blade**.)

Veins have two patterns, depending on the type of **flowering**

plant they are found in. In flowering plants that **germinate** with one leaf (like corn) (**monocotyledons**) there is a simple pattern of veins that do not branch, but simply grow up more or less parallel from the base of the leaf. In the case of plants that germinate with two leaves (**dicotyledons**) the veins form a branching pattern that covers the leaf with a network of fine lines. (*See also:* **Vascular plants** and **Vascular system**.)

Vine

A **plant** without a self-supporting **stem**. Vines climb up other plants and surfaces by making use of **tendrils** or by twisting themselves around the **stem** of another plant. Some vines also creep along the ground. These plants are often referred to as creepers. Vines include grapes, tomatoes and Virginia creeper.

W

Weed

Any **plant** that has grown unwanted in a cultivated plot like a garden or farm field.

Weeds are **native** plants, that is, they are plants that would have grown in an area when it was undisturbed. When land is cleared, weeds simply **colonise** the site, either because the cleared ground allows their **seeds** to **germinate**, or by sending out **runners** and underground **stems** (**rhizomes**).

Gardeners and farmers regard these successful native plants as pests because they compete for light and nourishment with the **cultivated plants**. In this way weeds reduce the growth of the cultivated plants.

Both **annual** seeds and plants that send out side stems are

difficult to remove entirely, even with herbicides. You can see this by the way in which a garden bed or a field rapidly becomes home to a variety of weeds when it is left untended for just a few weeks. (*See also:* **Reproduction**.)

Wilt

A drooping state of a **plant** when it has too little water to keep its **cells** under pressure (in a state of **turgor**). In general, a plant that wilts easily will recover quickly if it gets water as soon as wilting occurs. Plants that wilt slowly often do not respond to a new supply of water and may die.

Wood

A hard substance that forms within the **stems** of larger **perennial plants**, particularly **trees**. It forms the core of the **stem** and strengthens it.

There are many terms for different kinds of wood.

Most of the wood is made of dead **tissue**. The very core of the wood is called the pith. Surrounding it is the bulk of the wood, often called heartwood. It is separated from the outer, dead **bark** by a thin layer of growing tissue (sometimes called the inner bark, **cambium**, or sapwood).

Wood forms around the pith in a series of growth rings that mark a growing season. Each ring is made of an inner 'early', or 'spring', wood that is lighter in colour, softer and produced at the beginning of the growing season. The outer part of the ring, often called 'late wood' or 'summerwood', forms later in the growing season and is darker and harder (*see:* **Seasonal rings**). (*See also:* **Conifer, coniferous tree**; **Hardwood**; **Life cycle**; **Softwood**.)

Woodland

A small area of land covered with **woody** vegetation set among farmlands. Contrast with **forest**, which is a term for a much more extensive area of **trees**.

Woody plant

A woody stem differs from an **herbaceous** stem by growing a ring of wood and bark year after year. In an herbaceous plant the stem never thickens or becomes woody, but stays soft, slender and pliable. That is because the whole stem is used to transport sap. In a woody plant the living tubes that carry the sap (called xylem and phloem) are in a ring called the cambium just below the bark. Each year the woody plant grows new sap-transporting tubes in the cambium, while the previous year's xylem tubes become wood and the phloem tubes add to the bark.

X

Xylem

A special group of tubes inside a **plant stem** that conduct water and **nutrients** from the **roots** to the **leaves**. The leaves then manufacture **sugar**, which is sent to other parts of the plant through parallel **phloem** tubes. (*See also:* **Vascular system**.)

◄ **Wood** – A section through a mature tree trunk, showing (from the outside) the outer protective bark, the cambium just inside, the heartwood and the pith. There are 97 rings on this trunk, making its age just short of a century.

Pith

Bark

Sapwood

Cambium

Heartwood

Index